HUNTING
THE
WHITETAIL
DEER

HUNTING THE WHITETAIL DEER

by Russell Tinsley

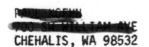
Outdoor Life · Harper & Row
New York

Manufactured in the United States of America

Contents

To my father, who taught me most of what I know
about deer hunting, and . . .
To my mother, who inspired me to put it down on paper.

1 The Abundant Whitetail

NO MATTER where you live in the United States, there is probably good whitetail deer hunting within a short drive of your home. The whitetail is literally everywhere, not only in the United States (where it is or has been found in all the continental states) but also in most of northern Mexico and southern Canada. This prolific animal is quite adaptable and can survive under almost all conditions and circumstances. That's why it is, by far, our most abundant and most popular big-game animal.

While much of our wildlife has dwindled before the march of civilization, the whitetail deer has thrived and multiplied. Today there are more whitetails roaming the land than ever before and it isn't unusual to sight them within the limits of some of our largest cities, even on the outskirts of New York City. There are so many deer, in fact, that overpopulations have become a serious problem in many areas.

In a scientific study, E. T. Atwood discovered more than 500 plants which the whitetail in the United States eats for forage. This is one reason why the whitetail has remained a dominant figure on our wildlife scene. Another reason is good protection by law. Still another, is the animal's ability to take advantage of almost any kind of terrain, from the flat, almost bare prairies to the heavily timbered hills.

I recall a time a few years back when I was quail hunting in an old, abandoned field in southern Alabama, near the town of Stockton, just above Mobile. The grass was about knee high, a solid carpet of it. My companion and I were slipping along, watching two ranging bird dogs half-hidden in the foliage ahead, when suddenly the dogs went on point. Half raising my shotgun, I advanced cautiously, expecting any moment the familiar whir of a quail rising into the air. But lo and behold, a whitetail deer suddenly jumped into sight and bounded away through the grass with those long, familiar, graceful leaps.

I discovered a bed of matted grass where the deer had been lying before we spooked it into the open. The field was surrounded by dense pine timber,

7

Our most abundant big-game animal, the whitetail is equally at home on the flat, bare prairies of the Southwest, the heavily wooded terrain of the Northeast or the swamplands of the Everglades.

and why the deer had chosen the tall grass for its mid-day bed, I don't know. But you'll often find deer in places where you least expect to see them.

Contrast this incident with the one which happened to me some time later. I was squirrel hunting at the time in southern Missouri, below Joplin in the foothills of the Ozark Mountains. While pussyfooting through the heavily timbered woods, I eased around a cluster of sycamore saplings and surprised two feeding deer. I could almost have reached out and touched them and I don't know which was the more startled, me or the deer.

These were the two extremes of terrain, open, overgrown field and dense, timbered woods, and whitetail deer can be found in just about every kind of imaginable cover between the two. In states such as Maine, Oregon, Michigan and Pennsylvania, you'll find whitetails roaming hills and mountains covered with hardwood trees; in the Everglades of Florida they inhabit a terrain that is virtually all water and where conservation officers must use airboats to make periodic checks on them; in the plantation country of Concordia Parish in Louisiana, they'll be seen in the table-flat country under huge oak trees draped with Spanish moss; and in the Mexican state of Sonora, across the border from Arizona, they roam an arid, cactus-covered desert.

This, then, is the whitetail deer, a very adaptable animal which can learn to live and reproduce in almost any environment, from the cold, wet climate of the mountains to the dry, stifling heat of the desert.

Basically, however, the whitetail is a fairly predictable animal, as wild creatures go. It prefers woody terrain, stealing out of the timber late in the evening to feed on into the night, returning to the cover the following morning to bed down during the daylight hours. It usually spends its lifetime in a pretty limited area, less than a square mile. Around abandoned apple orchards in Washington and Oregon, you'll find whitetails coming out of the surrounding woods into the orchards early and late in the day. The same is true in Texas where as the sun sinks toward the western horizon deer steal out of the woods to feed, particularly in the lush green oats fields. Dr. William B. Davis, writing in a Texas Parks and Wildlife Department bulletin titled "The Mammals of Texas," points out that it has been found by experiment that deer are most easily observed in the hour just before dark.

The whitetail deer found throughout the United States, in Canada and Mexico, is one and the same animal, even though the whitetail in Georgia may vary greatly in size from its counterpart in Maine, and those in northern Missouri will be larger on the average than those found in southern Missouri. Size ranges from the occasional 200-pounds-plus specimens found in Missouri, Wisconsin, Michigan and Maine, to the diminutive and rare Key deer, weighing less than seventy pounds, which are restricted to a few islands lying off the coast of southern Florida.

Several years ago, I had occasion to hunt whitetail deer in the neighboring states of New Mexico and Texas within a time span of two weeks. In the Lincoln National Forest of New Mexico, I bagged a forkhorn which field-dressed 118 pounds; a week later I killed a forkhorn near the small community of Mason in central Texas which field-dressed a mere fifty-eight pounds. Yet the antler size of the two animals was almost identical. There was that much variance in weight even though the two animals belonged basically to the same sub-species.

In all, there are nine or ten recognized sub-species, depending which authority you believe. The *Hunter's Encyclopedia* lists ten different sub-species: the Virginia deer, Eastern whitetail deer, Northern Virginia deer, Key deer, Coues deer, Louisiana deer, Plains whitetail, Northwestern whitetail, Florida whitetail and Texas whitetail. The most abundant is the typical Eastern whitetail deer, found from Virginia up through Pennsylvania and New York to Maine.

But despite the different sub-species grouped within the entire whitetail family, the deer looks practically the same no matter where you meet it. The Maine deer hunter would immediately recognize the Florida whitetail as the same animal he hunts back in the north woods. The only noticeable difference would be in size. The antlers of the whitetail, unlike the mule deer, have all the points growing off two main beams. The tail has the familiar white underside, which has come to be called the "white flag" because a scared whitetail has a habit of tossing the tail straight up and waving the white back and forth as it runs. All whitetails have the same general coloring, brownish in fall and winter, reddish in summer.

The antlers of whitetails also will vary in size in different parts of the country. Biologists say the mineral content of the soil where deer range is the determining factor as far as antler size is concerned. For instance, in southern Texas, a brushy region from which many record heads have come, the general size of the antlers will be much larger than those on deer in neighboring Louisiana and Arkansas. A deer with four points on either antler will be called an eight-pointer in the East, but in the West hunters know it as a three-pointer (only the points on one antler are counted, disregarding the brow point). An average mature whitetail deer has from six to ten points, generally eight—six main points, three on either beam, and two brow points, one growing out of each beam just above the head.

The whitetail is a very cunning and sly animal, a real challenge to hunters. Many nimrods claim it is our most elusive big-game animal. It is a master of the disappearing act, slipping out of the thickest cover without a give-away sound. Yet it also can run swiftly when spooked into the open.

Many hunters can walk into a section of woods heavily populated with deer, roam around for several days, and come out believing that there hasn't been one of the critters within miles. I once knew a man who spent two days hunting on Manitoulin Island, which lies in the northern part of Lake Huron and boasts a considerable population of whitetails, and never saw one of the critters. He said only the betraying tracks revealed that deer were there at all. A whitetail won't dash into the open, showing itself, unless it absolutely must. It would much rather catfoot away quietly, slipping around until it is well out of hearing before it bolts for freedom.

I had the opportunity to watch such a drama a few years ago in south-central New Mexico, near the village of Piñon. I was sitting on a butte-like

Despite the various sub-species distributed throughout the country, the whitetail is basically the same animal no matter where you find him. The antlers are characterized by two main beams, each with a number of points—from six to ten in mature bucks. The tail is white on the underside, and the coloring is brownish in fall and winter, reddish in summer. *Courtesy Texas Game and Fish Commission*

hill overlooking a wide, shallow draw, hunkered down on an outcropping of rock while my two hunting companions stalked through the piñons and brush, moving slowly, watching and listening.

Suddenly I glimpsed movement out in front of Clarence Brown. I lifted my binoculars and looked. A large whitetail buck was slipping ahead of him, far enough ahead so that he was shielded from the hunter by a wall of brush. The buck didn't hurry. He stayed just far enough ahead to escape detection.

There was no chance for a shot without endangering Clarence, so I merely watched curiously. The buck moved along ahead of the hunter for perhaps one hundred feet before cutting off at an angle, ghosting through the brush. He circled around, got behind the hunter, ducked into another clump of brush and practically vanished. His dark coat blended perfectly with his habitat. Only occasionally could I catch a fleeting glimpse of movement as he made good his retreat. There wasn't a chance for a shot.

This is typical of the whitetail. It has an uncanny sense of knowing which route to take, away from danger. Seldom will one, frightened, run straight to or away from the hunter. Instead, it cuts away, using every bit of available cover to handicap its pursuer during its escape.

Once, while hunting in this same area of New Mexico, I sighted a large herd of deer moving along the opposite side of a wide and shallow canyon. I studied the deer through my binoculars. One was an exceptionally large buck, a real trophy.

I watched the deer as they walked along the rim, silhouetted by the morning sun. Perhaps one hundred yards farther along they dropped off into the canyon, quartering across at a tangent. I mentally laid out a course they would follow, and backtracked until I was hidden by trees, then ran, bent double, as fast as I could without making undue commotion to a point of brush which would give me vantage overlooking the deer's route, within one hundred yards of where they would likely pass.

Just as I slipped into the wedge of brush, one of the tail-end deer in the procession caught the unnatural movement. The doe snorted alarmingly. It would seem logical that a noise from behind would have pushed the deer ahead, along the same route they were following. But instead, they flared off in all directions like a flushed covey of quail and bolted into the brushy innards of the canyon. The dozen or more whitetails disappeared as quickly and completely as if they'd been passed over by a magician's wand.

The whitetail deer's basic line of defense is its sensitive smelling apparatus and sonar-like hearing. It also possesses extremely sharp eyesight, but it depends primarily on smelling and hearing to protect it against its enemies. A domestic cow can walk through the woods, right up on a deer without the wild animal becoming alarmed; but let a hunter try the same thing, and the deer will readily notice the difference in the footsteps.

But despite this omnipresent cunningness bred into the whitetail, the animal can be quickly tamed when handled correctly. I've seen many that made gentle pets, particularly those raised in captivity from fawns. And mature deer can become fairly tame, even if they had no contact with civilization until they became adults.

I witnessed a rare sight a few years back on the Dolores Ranch, about twenty miles outside the city of Laredo on the Texas-Mexico border. The ranch, with only a small natural deer population of its own, had been liberally stocked with deer from the sprawling King Ranch. These deer, adapted to the abundant foodstuffs found on the King Ranch, of race-horse fame, were hard pressed to survive on the cactus-covered, almost grassless countryside near Laredo. From the time the adult deer were released, ranch hands supplemented their natural diet with cattle feed. Every evening a cowboy would go to a site near a stock pond, rattling a bucket and scattering the feed. Almost immediately, deer would start materializing out of the brush, several dozen of them. There was everything from young does and spike bucks to old bucks with bragging-sized racks of antlers. The deer would crowd around the ranch hand, feeding, oblivious to any onlookers who came to gaze upon the spectacle. It was almost like feeding a herd of domestic cattle.

The mating season of the deer, or "rut" as it is more commonly called, occurs in the fall, triggered by cold weather. Usually the first abrupt drop in temperature, down close to freezing, will start the deer to mating. During this time, closely watch any gathering of does since a buck is almost sure to be nearby. The neck of the buck will swell considerably and his glands will give off a strong odor. Bucks will fight amongst themselves for the affection of a lady friend, squaring off to clash their antlers together, pawing the ground and snorting. On rare occasions the antlers will become hopelessly locked together and the deer will perish of starvation.

After a gestation of about seven months, the doe will drop either one or two fawns. Sexual maturity in a doe usually isn't reached until she is eighteen months of age, or the second fall after birth. Her first offspring is apt to be a single fawn, but after that it is quite common for her to bear twins. The young will lie low, depending for safety on their natural camouflage, while the mother ranges several hundred feet in either direction to feed. But as soon as they are able to move about, she will take them with her. Normally, they are weaned in early fall when they also lose their telltale spots and take on the more familiar brownish hue.

The buck sheds his antlers every year. There seems to be a direct correlation between testicular activity and the growth and losing of antlers in a whitetail buck. When the testes are inactive, after the rut, the deer loses his antlers. They simply fall off, leaving two reddish stubs that are even with the head hair. Soon thereafter, they begin growing again, being covered with a mosslike substance called velvet. These antlers are the fastest growing bone known. When the rut nears and the sexual glands begin to activate, the

The mating season occurs in the fall at the onset of cold weather. Bucks fight among themselves for the does, often trail their prospective mate for miles through the woods.

Fawns are born in the spring and remain under the mother's care until early fall when they lose their telltale spots and take on the brownish hue of the adult deer. *Courtesy Texas Game and Fish Commission*

antlers become hardened and the bucks rub the velvet off against sapling trees. The scraped trees are called "deer rubs."

When a deer's sexual glands are damaged, as by castration when jumping over a fence or pierced by thorns, the deer never loses the velvet covering, the antlers never become solid, and the antlers take on all kinds of weird shapes. These deer with the velvet antlers are known as "stags." And for some inexplicable reason, a few deer seem to be born without any male organs, even though they have all the other visible features of bucks, even the antlers. But in this case the antlers never develop properly and the bucks never lose their velvet. In some rare instances even does grow antlers. I once saw a doe bagged near Canoe Creek in northeast Pennsylvania which carried a nice eight-point rack of antlers.

No one can explain logically this inexplicable mixup of nature when a doe acquires an antlered headset except that something went wrong biologically. The antlers are fully developed, free of velvet.

Contrary to popular thought, the age of a deer can not be accurately determined by the size of his antlers. A grandpa buck, in his declining years, may sport no larger a headset than an eighteen-month-old deer. Dr. Roger Latham, now outdoors editor of the Pittsburgh (Pa.) *Press* but once a long-time biologist with the Pennsylvania Game and Fish Commission, says a properly developed second-year deer should have at least forked antlers, perhaps even six or eight points. Small hardened spikes protruding through the skin indicate the deer isn't healthy or isn't properly developed. This family-

14

A whitetail buck with velvet still on his antlers. Antler growth begins in April or May; as the rut approaches the velvet is shed; and the antlers drop off in late December or January. This cycle is repeated every year in healthy bucks. *Courtesy Texas Game and Fish Commission*

tree characteristic can be bred into other deer. Large antlers are the result partly of heredity, partly of nutrition.

A hunter with no formal training can estimate the age of whitetails to about two years of age by examining the teeth. The fawn will acquire its middle pair of permanent incisors at about nine months, while the remainder of the incisors and the premolars will be milk teeth, tiny in size. By eighteen months of age, the milk teeth will be replaced by permanent teeth. At least two of the molars are fully developed, while the third will shortly emerge. By two years, the permanent teeth are acquired. From then on, only a qualified wildlife biologist can accurately gauge a deer's age by noting the wear on teeth. At about five years old, the ridges of a deer's teeth no longer are sharp, having been worn until they rise only slightly above the dentine.

The dramatic upsurge of whitetail deer populations within the past few decades can be attributed to several factors. Good conservation measures and sound protective legislation are two of them. Another is the practice of cleaning out underbrush and allowing young trees to grow, providing more browse. In places today it is common practice to trap deer and transplant them to areas of limited or no population. Mostly baited wooden traps are used, but on the swampy Delta Wildlife Refuge in southern Louisiana, the deer are captured through the use of helicopters and airboats, of all things. After being moved to suitable habitat, the deer usually thrive and multiply.

One of the first moves to conserve our deer was the inauguration of deer seasons. Before the turn of the century, the deer was mostly unprotected. But about 1900 the first game laws were passed. In Pennsylvania, for example, there were only about 200 deer killed in 1907. By 1923 this number had risen to 6,452 legal bucks. In 1940 more than 30,000 were killed. Today, Pennsylvania ranks as one of our leading deer-producing states.

In many places not enough deer are removed from the available habitat. This has prompted one of the latest innovations to eliminate surplus deer, the controlled killing of doe or antlerless deer. In states today which have general deer seasons, there are 23 which allow only the killing of bucks and 22 which provide for the taking of deer of either sex. This excepts some states like Rhode Island, which allows only bow-and-arrow hunting, and Illinois and Indiana which limit their deer hunting to residents only. Many of the states have gone to plans like the one in Vermont that allows hunters to take antlerless deer or ones with antlers not over three inches in length one day of the year, this by law being the first Saturday in December. Pennsylvania has a similar plan with a "doe day" when licenses are apportioned out by counties. Washington is divided into game units with some units having permit drawings for does and others having shorter either-sex seasons. Most other states use either of these systems to take surplus deer from limited areas of over-population. The trend, however, seems to be toward a general either-sex season in most of the major deer-producing states.

This, then, is the story of the whitetail deer, the No. 1 wildlife success story of the past century, our No. 1 big-game hunting animal, the pride and joy of deer hunters everywhere.

WHAT WILL IT WEIGH?

Dressed weight in pounds	Live weight in pounds	Dressed weight in pounds	Live weight in pounds
40	55	130	165
50	65	140	180
60	80	150	190
70	90	160	205
80	105	170	215
90	115	180	230
100	130	190	240
110	140	200	255
120	155	210	265

2 Choosing the Deer Cartridge

THERE IS no "best" deer gun, one that will adequately cover all needs and circumstances. The weapon for hunting whitetail deer is an individual and personal thing, based on each hunter's particular needs. A nimrod after deer in the Pocono Mountains of northeast Pennsylvania wouldn't want or need the same type of rifle used by a hunter after whitetails in the Devil's Nest area of Nebraska's Knox County. The former is heavy timber where shots normally will be at extremely close range; the latter is more open country, with rolling hills, where longer shots are probable.

There are several considerations to keep in mind when shopping for a deer weapon: type of terrain where you'll be hunting, whether or not you're a beginning or experienced hunter, state laws, how good a shot you are, whether it will be a deer gun exclusively or will be utilized for many different types of game.

When speaking of the deer gun, we are referring basically to calibers. The choice of an action is more a personal preference (*see next chapter*). Whether you pick a bolt action, slide action, lever action or semi-automatic isn't really important. What is important is that you select the kind of action that suits you best, learn to use it and stick with it.

The most popular deer load of all is the time-honored .30/30. In the hands of a fairly competent shooter this cartridge is more than adequate for whitetail deer. I've killed many deer with the .30/30, most of them one-shot kills. In fact, my first deer gun was a .30/30, and of the first five bucks I bagged, four were killed with the .30/30. The one big advantage of the .30/30 is that it is so commonplace that you can find ammunition for your rifle no matter where you may be. This is one cartridge that all sporting goods stores stock.

The .30/30 has enjoyed phenomenal popularity even though it isn't what you'd call a long-range cartridge. It performs best at ranges of up to 150 yards. The reason for its continued popularity, of course, is that most whitetails, in fact more than 80 per cent, are bagged at a range of less than one hundred yards. The very nature of the whitetails' habitat, in most cases, calls for short-range shooting and a bullet that can plough through the brush without being deflected off target.

Naturally there are exceptions. It is up to each hunter to evaluate his own situation and needs and get a gun that will do the job for him. This means a complete outfit—rifle, cartridge and sight. And don't forget to have your state laws in mind when picking a deer cartridge. A few states prohibit anything smaller than .25 caliber for deer.

Just about any big-game rifle can be used for deer hunting. The .30/06 and .270, two long-time favorites, are both popular, although the deer hunter really doesn't require a cartridge this powerful. But it is always best to be overpowered rather than underpowered. This way a shot that may be off its mark a few inches can still deliver a fatal punch, preventing needless crippling and waste of game.

It is difficult to pinpoint the *minimum* deer load. Anything smaller than the .250 Savage should be ruled out. For the experienced hunter and expert shot, the .250 Savage and .257 Roberts will be sufficient, but the less experienced may need something drastically more potent, like the .30/06 and .308. The average hunter, an adequate hunter and adequate shot but nothing extraordinary, can get by with something like the .30/30 and .243.

Production rifles for both the .250 Savage and .257 Roberts have been discontinued, but if you can pick up a used firearm in good shape for either of these calibers, don't hestitate to do so. Both were—and still are—excellent calibers for whitetail deer.

The trend nowadays is to high velocity. More and more cartridges are showing up on the market that are "souped up." This added velocity has several advantages. For one, it makes for flatter bullet trajectory and consequently better bullet placement, especially at longer ranges when hunting in more open country like that found in the northern Mexican state of Sonora, across from Arizona. For another, the high velocity bullets kill better, since a bullet kills by shock. The one big disadvantage of a high-velocity bullet is that it is easily sidetracked by brush, while a slower and bigger bullet, like the .35 Remington, will plough its way right through. But personally, I'd rather sacrifice this brush-penetrating ability for the higher velocity.

My vote for the best all-around whitetail cartridges are the .243 and 6mm. The 100-grain bullet of the .243 Winchester leaves the muzzle at a velocity of 3,070 feet-per-second, while that of the 6mm Remington, same 100-grain size, is 3,190. Both bullets have sufficient sectional density for good killing power. Sectional density is the ratio of bullet length to diameter. Length in a bullet is always desirable for better results. The added length means better accuracy, more sustained velocity and more striking force. Of two bullets, one of .25 caliber and another of .30 caliber, which weigh the same, the .25-caliber will give the better performance simply because of the smaller bore diameter which means the .25 bullet must necessarily be longer. For instance, a 100-grain bullet in the .243 would be more desirable than a comparable 100-grain bullet in the .30/06.

The rifles for the .243 and 6mm are lightweight, making for fast handling, a definite asset in most whitetail deer hunting. These cartridges are fairly dependable in light brush, yet also are good at the extreme ranges, 200 yards and up.

However, in heavier brush you may want to select a bullet with more weight and stubbier, to get through the cover. The shooter will be sacrificing velocity, but it isn't really needed for the close-range brush shooting. Most hunters seen around the Catskill Mountains of New York will be using weapons chambered for the .30/30 and .35 Remington. The Ruger Carbine, chambered for the .44 Magnum cartridge, was designed specifically for close-range brush shooting. The cartridge, like the .35 Remington, will plough through the brush rather than ricocheting.

One main gripe against the bigger calibers, such as the .30/06 and .308, is that they destroy too much meat. The truth is, though, that any bullet is going to destroy meat when it hits an animal in a vital area. The .30/06 naturally will destroy more tissue than the .30/30, but there is the advantage of having more killing power when the bullet placement isn't where it is supposed to be. A whitetail hit in the flank with a .30/06 bullet isn't going far; however, one struck in the same general vicinity with a .30/30 may escape to die a slow lingering death in the woods.

What this all boils down to is that each hunter must buy a deer gun to suit his individual needs. This will be his "best" gun for deer hunting. Generally, the most popular whitetail deer calibers are those in the .250 Savage to .30/06 and .308 range, with the .30/30, 6mm and .243 being the mean.

A good basic rule to follow is to go to the heavier bullets, like the .35 Remington, .30/06 (180-grain bullet) and .44 Magnum for dense brush shooting, the flatter-trajectory cartridges like the .243 and 6mm for hunting in more sparsely timbered areas where there is lighter cover and shots are apt to be longer.

For hunting in heavy brush and dense timber, a shotgun frequently is the logical choice (all but five of the forty-eight states which have deer seasons allow the use of shotguns, but only twenty-three permit the use of buckshot). In some states such as Delaware, Ohio, Indiana, Illinois, Iowa, Massachusetts, and New Jersey, law dictates that only shotguns can be used for deer hunting. The shotgun also is popular in some other states, as in St. Martin's Parish, in the Louisiana Cajun country, where deer are hunted with dogs, and shots usually are at close range with the deer running. The shotgun is one of the deadliest of all weapons at close range, delivering a powerful wallop.

The shotgun, armed with solid-slug shotshells, also is good in brush shooting because of brush penetration with the big, blunt projectiles. If your deer will be at close range and probably running, buckshot, if legal, is the choice, since you can swing and aim at the deer instinctively. But it is wise to use slugs for the second or even third shot, since the deer is farther off.

The scattergun is a limited weapon in deer hunting. No. 0 shot is effective to about fifty yards, with 00 reaching out to sixty yards. Rifled slugs are deadly to seventy-five yards and can give rifle-like precision in a gun equipped with proper sights (some hunters even put low-power scopes on their shotguns).

Buckshot is safer in populous areas in that pellets quickly lose their energy and have less killing range. No. 0 and 00 shot are available only in 12 gauge since they don't pattern well in the smaller gauges. There will be nine pellets of 00 shot in a conventional 12-gauge shell and twelve No. 0 pellets. Magnum loads will contain twelve of No. 00 in the 2¾-inch shell and fifteen in the 3-inch Magnum. Any full choke 12-gauge gun is satisfactory for deer hunting if it will pattern half of its shot within a thirty-inch circle at fifty yards. When shooting buckshot aim at the deer's head and neck. A body-shot deer is apt to run for miles.

Rifled slugs come in .410, 20, 16 and 12 gauges. In muzzle velocity and energy, the slugs compare favorably with the heavier rifle bullets used in brush shooting, although they can't match the accuracy. A rifled shotgun slug leaves the muzzle with a velocity of 1,600 feet-per-second in 12 gauge and with 2,400 foot-pounds of energy. It holds up well, too, for fifty yards, still having 1,370 fps of energy in retained velocity.

Since many shotguns won't group slugs with deer-killing accuracy, all of the major firearms manufacturers now have special shotguns designed for slug shooting. These are not new models, but rather modifications of standard production guns. Typical are the Ithaca Model 37 "Deerslayer" and Remington Model 870 "Brushmaster." The barrels have no choke to speak of, the muzzle being of standard diameter throughout the length of the barrel. They come equipped with standard adjustable open sights. A regular shotgun barrel can be substituted for the special slug barrel when bird hunting. The High-Standard Deluxe "Deer Buster" has, on the other hand, a Williams receiver peep sight (the standard model comes with open sights). Most of these models come with 20- to 22-inch barrels for fast handling in the brush, and they'll hold into a four-inch group at fifty yards.

But picking the gun itself is only the first step in successful deer hunting. Equally important is the type of sight that will be used on the gun.

Most all production rifles come from the factory equipped with standard open sights. This type of sight is the fastest of all to use and it is extremely popular with brush shooters. But open sights come in many designs and shapes, most of them bad. The shallow V's and U's, ones that the sighter can see through and get down in, are the best. The tendency with the open sight is for the hunter to overshoot, because he isn't getting down in the sight properly. The worst open sights are the buckhorn types, with the wrap-around tops that look good but serve no useful purpose except to cut out light and keep the hunter from sighting properly.

The open sight also has a range limitation. Up to one hundred yards it is fairly adequate, but at ranges of 200 yards and more, it is practically worthless.

The person who buys an expensive big-game rifle should be willing to lay out some more cash to get a good sight. After all, a rifle can't hit its mark unless the bullet is guided accurately. The peep sight is better, economical and almost as fast as open sights. First thing to do with a peep is to unscrew the disc with the small aperture and throw it away. Only the large screw hole

The peep sight is fast and accurate, especially in brush country where the shooter has to pull down on a deer before it vanishes in the undergrowth. It has micrometer adjustments for elevation and windage.

remains; aim through this. Just because you can command a wide view of countryside through the larger opening doesn't mean it won't be accurate. On the contrary. It will be just as accurate as the small aperture, and at the same time it will be quicker and easier to use. For a front sight, pick an even post in a color that can be distinguished under most conditions. Red is exceptionally good. Ivory also is acceptable.

The peep is extremely accurate up to one hundred yards and beyond. In the brush, the experienced shooter can pull down on a running deer almost as fast with the peep as he can with open sights. The big drawback to the peep is that it is often placed too close to the eye for absolutely safe use on a recoiling big-game rifle. There's always the outside chance the sight may get jammed back into the eye.

The best all-purpose sight, as far as I'm concerned, is the telescope. It is a lifesaver for the person with failing eyesight. It also makes for more precise bullet placement and, in some instances, takes the place of binoculars for proper game identification. The scope is a fairly good sight even for brush shooting and running shots when the hunter gets used to it.

The 4X, or four power, scope probably is the best all-around sight for deer hunting. It is exceptionally adaptable to longer shooting, for use as an emergency spotting scope, and passable as a brush sight. But it isn't fast enough to use in real dense cover. My friend Tom Hayes, a long-time deer hunter with experience in many states, has a versatile outfit which includes a four-power scope and a quick-detachable peep sight. The peep is carried in his cartridge belt. If the sudden need arises, he can quickly dismount the scope, ram the peep into place and be ready for close, fast shooting.

For close-range and snap shooting, the 2½X scope is much superior to the 4X. The lower powered sight has more light-gathering capabilities, has a wider field of view and a greater latitude of eye relief—all advantages when hunting in heavy cover.

Despite what you may have heard to the contrary, a scope is extremely fast for picking up running game, particularly in medium to sparse cover. It just takes a little getting used to. The one big advantage of it is that the shooter has to line up only two objects, the crosshairs of the scope and the target. Everything appears in the same plane. On the alternatives, the open and peep

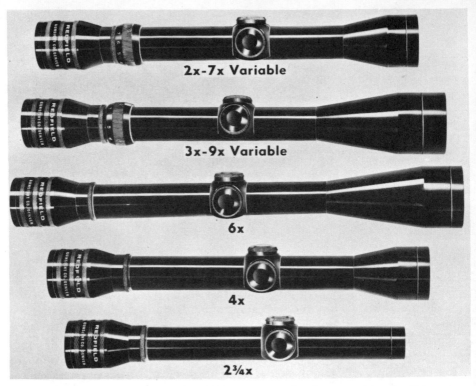

2x-7x Variable

3x-9x Variable

6x

4x

2¾x

Telescope sights are available in a variety of powers. The deer hunter could use a 4X in most situations; a 2½X is better for snap shooting in dense cover. Variable power scopes are useful, but only with crosshairs; a dot or post reticule tends to get larger as you increase power.

sights, he must align the back and front sights, as well as the target. And of these two, the peep is quicker because the front sight is just placed on the target as it is centered in the aperture.

But the scope does have some disadvantages. For one thing the field of view is limited. With open or peep sights, the shooter, accustomed to getting on the animal with both eyes open, can immediately pick up his target. The scope takes just a little longer. And in heavy cover the so-called "picket effect" might distract the aim. This effect is caused by the deer running through trees with cover between the animal and shooter. The trees flash across the scope and it is almost like trying to aim through a picket fence.

Actually, the choice of a sight will vary with the terrain. Under most circumstances, I recommend the scope. In heavy brush, where shots will be real close and often running, I think the peep is best. It is a matter of weighing the advantages of a particular sight against the disadvantages. The main drawbacks to the scope are that on a deer standing close, the shooter may see nothing but hair, making it difficult to pinpoint the bullet accurately; and on close, running deer it takes a split-second longer to pick the animal up and get on it. But I can count on my fingers the number of running deer I have killed; yet it would require all my fingers and toes, plus some, to count those I have missed. Hitting a fleeing deer requires real skill. A scant few of us have the ability to put the bullet in a vital area. All too often we simply shoot at the entire deer. This is inviting crippled game. For this reason I recommend the scope sight. It is far better not even to get a shot at a deer when you're not sure of putting the bullet in a killing spot than to "throw lead" and hope the bullet somehow finds its mark. The hallmark of the topflight deer hunter is his being able to ambush the quarry without first being detected, to work for shots within the realm of his ability and to try to make that first shot count every time. It seems foolhardy to me to select a particular sight just because the shooter *might* get a chance at a running deer. Take the positive approach, I say, and use the sight that will perform best under the most circumstances. Play the odds. And the best all-purpose sight, I repeat, is the scope.

If you might be hunting in heavy cover, however, and need a fast sight for close shooting and will take the time to learn how to use it for optimum results, then consider the peep-scope combination. With practice, the shooter can remove the scope and substitute the peep in mere seconds. Thus in more open country he can employ the scope; the peep is the choice for heavy cover. The scope also is handicapped in rain or mist and this is another obvious advantage of having an auxiliary sight like the detachable peep in reserve. Otherwise, cradle the scope under your waterproof jacket until you're prepared to shoot.

So the hunter after whitetail deer would evaluate his needs and pick either the 4X sight or one of lower power, the lowest possible, which is 2½X in most scopes, for heavier cover. But simply picking the needed power is only part of the job. Just as important is the reticule. The common crosshair is fairly standard but the crossing lines don't project plainly enough for quick shooting. Best of all is the post reticule. This gives the impression of shooting with open sights, and the post shows up readily to the hunter pulling down on game.

The post for short-range shooting, like that in typical whitetail deer country, should be large enough to stand out boldly, something with a flat top with a slope of about four to six minutes of angle. The horizontal crosshair is optional, although I prefer to have it.

Another good reticule for fast shooting is the dot. But again, the dot should be large and bold so that the shooter can readily pick it up when he's trying to get off a fast shot, about a four-to-six-minute dot. The main drawback to either the post or dot is that it tends to cover up the target at long ranges, but since most whitetails are shot at ranges of less than eighty yards, this isn't a serious handicap unless you plan on using your rifle for several purposes, from long-range varmint shooting to deer hunting. In this case it might be wise to have interchangeable scopes, one of high power for varmint shooting and a low-power job for deer. Trying to make one fixed-power scope serve several widely diversified tasks is only defeating your basic purpose.

But the scope is more than just a device for lining up on a deer. In early morning and late afternoon, two prime times for seeing deer, and also on dark overcast days when the light is bad, a quality scope has light-gathering power. A shooter often can place a bullet pretty accurately with a scope when

Three of the most common types of reticules (from left): crosshairs, post, dot. For under eighty yards, the post or dot are recommended as they show up clearly when the hunter has to get off a fast shot.

there is not enough light even to see open sights, much less aim with them.

I remember a time when my dad, O. D. Tinsley, and I discovered just how valuable a scope can be under such adverse conditions. We were heading back to where we'd parked our auto one dark, overcast November day, after hunting through the day without seeing a legal buck. The premature dark was quickly settling over the countryside and we were hurrying to beat darkness.

We were walking briskly down a game trail, not paying any particular attention to anything around us, when suddenly a commotion in a nearby clump of oak saplings brought us to an abrupt halt. We squinted our eyes and looked intently, trying to make out in the fading light what had caused the ruckus.

About then a nice buck ran out of the trees, trotted up the side of a hill and paused about eighty yards away. "Take him," Dad instructed softly.

I raised my .30/30 with open sights and tried to pull down on the buck. But the sights blurred and I couldn't make shape out of shadow.

"I can't, I can't," I whispered hoarsely. "Too dark to see."

Dad quickly raised his .300 Savage with the 4X Weaver scope, steadied the weapon and squeezed the trigger. At the muzzle blast, the six-pointer (Eastern count) dropped heavily. The slug had entered just where Dad was aiming, right beyond the shoulders.

Without the aid of a scope we'd never have gotten that buck.

The scope sight also has the ability almost to "see" through brush. This penetrating trait is a definite asset to the whitetail deer hunter.

For the hunter seeking a compromise, there are variable scopes available which can be adjusted to include several ranges of power. My father used one for years, quite successfully, that went from 2½X to 5X. He employed the lower power for brush shooting; the stronger power for shots that were likely to be longer. But the variable is only good with crosshairs; with the post or large dot, you run into a problem as you increase the power, since the reticule tends to get larger. If you don't mind the handicap of the finer crosshairs, a variable might be the scope for you. There are many good ones on the market. Earlier models tended to be bulky, but the modern variable isn't much larger than a fixed-power scope.

Many deer hunters like to equip their weapons with swing-away scope mounts. This way the open factory sights can be left intact, and should occasion present itself, the scope sight can be quickly flipped over so that the open sights can be pressed into duty. This fast access is nice should the hunter need the open sights for close-range shooting, or perhaps he would prefer the detachable peep sight mentioned earlier. Some available scope mounts have back open sights built into the base. Standard top mounts make the use of factory sights impractical since part of the base remains on the rifle receiver even when the scope is detached.

But the ruggedness of today's scopes makes the need for auxiliary sights questionable. They are nice in the rare times when you need them, but the average deer hunter could get by with the scope and no more, in most parts of the country. It takes quite a blow to put a modern scope out of commission; so about the only needs for the iron auxiliary sights would be for close, snap shooting and during a rain.

If I had to have only one sight I would undoubtedly pick the scope. Anything else would be an auxiliary sight, nothing more. I'm convinced that the advantages of the scope far outweigh the disadvantages, and that the scope definitely scores higher on all things you look for in a sight than either the peep or open sights. A scope sight makes a good shooter an even better shot, and it assures more clean kills and less cripples.

SHOTGUN BALLISTICS

Rifled Slugs

Gauge	Shell Length	Slug Weight ounces	Velocity muzzle	50 yds.	100 yds.	Energy foot pounds muzzle	50 yds.	100 yds.
410	2½ inches	⅕	1,830	1,335	1,025	650	345	205
28	2¾	½	1,600	1,175	950	1,245	670	440
20	2½	⅝	1,600	1,175	950	1,555	840	550
16	2¾	⅞	1,600	1,175	950	2,175	1,175	765
12	2¾	1	1,600	1,175	950	2,485	1,350	875

Drop in Inches

Gauge	25 yds.	50 yds.	100 yds.
410	.4	1.6	8.2
28	.5	2.1	10.4
20	.5	2.1	10.4
16	.5	2.1	10.4
12	.5	2.1	10.4

Pellets

Gauge	Shell Length	Number of Pellets	Velocity muzzle	20 yds.	50 yds.	Energy foot pounds muzzle	20 yds.	50 yds.
12	2¾"	12 of No. 0	1,300	1,120	960	140	100	70
12	3"	15 of No. 00	1,250	1,085	940	185	140	105
12	2¾"	12 of No. 00	1,325	1,135	970	210	155	110
12	2¾"	9 of No. 00	1,325	1,135	970	210	155	110

Drop in Inches

Gauge	Shell Length	Number of Pellets	20 yds.	50 yds.
12	2¾"	12 of No. 0	.5	3.3
12	3"	15 of No. 00	.5	3.5
12	2¾"	12 of No. 00	.4	3.2
12	2¾"	9 of No. 00	.4	3.2

(All tabulations made for full choke, 30-inch barrel)

BALLISTICS OF MOST POPULAR DEER CARTRIDGES

Cartridge	Bullet wgt. grains	Bullet type	Velocity ft. per sec. muzzle	Velocity ft. per sec. 100 yds.	Energy foot pounds muzzle	Energy foot pounds 100 yds.	Mid-range trajectory 100 yds.	200	300
6mm Remington	100	Exp.	3,190	2,920	2,260	1,890	0.5	2.1	6.5
.243 Winchester	100	S.P.	3,070	2,790	2,090	1,730	0.5	2.2	5.5
.257 Roberts	100	Exp.	2,900	2,540	1,870	1,430	0.6	2.9	7.4
.257 Roberts	117	S.P.	2,650	2,280	1,820	1,350	0.7	3.4	8.8
.270 Winchester	100	S.P.	3,580	3,160	2,840	2,210	0.4	1.7	4.5
.270 Winchester	130	Exp.	3,140	2,850	2,840	2,340	0.5	2.1	5.3
.270 Winchester	150	S.P.	2,800	2,400	2,610	1,920	0.7	3.0	7.8
7mm Mauser (7X57)	175	S.P.	2,490	2,170	2,410	1,830	0.8	3.7	9.5
.280 Remington	150	Exp.	2,810	2,580	2,630	2,220	0.6	2.6	6.5
.284 Winchester	125	S.P.	3,200	2,880	2,840	2,300	0.5	2.1	5.3
.284 Winchester	150	S.P.	2,800	2,630	2,800	2,300	0.6	2.5	6.3
.30/30 Winchester	150	Exp.	2,410	2,020	1,930	1,360	0.9	4.2	11.0
.30/30 Winchester	170	S.P. & Exp.	2,220	1,890	1,860	1,350	1.2	4.6	12.5
.30 Remington	170	S.P. & Exp.	2,220	1,890	1,860	1,350	1.2	4.6	12.5
.30/40 Krag	180	S.P. & Exp.	2,470	2,120	2,440	1,790	0.8	3.8	9.9
.30/40 Krag	220	Exp.	2,200	1,990	2,360	1,930	1.0	4.4	11.0
.30/06 Springfield	110	S.P.	3,420	2,880	2,850	2,020	0.4	2.1	5.6
.30/06 Springfield	150	Exp.	2,970	2,670	2,930	2,370	0.6	2.4	6.1
.30/06 Springfield	180	Exp.	2,700	2,470	2,910	2,440	0.7	2.9	7.0
.30/06 Springfield	220	S.P.	2,410	2,120	2,830	2,190	0.8	3.9	9.8
.300 Savage	150	S.P.	2,670	2,350	2,370	1,840	0.7	3.2	8.0
.300 Savage	180	Exp.	2,370	2,160	2,240	1,860	0.9	3.7	9.2
.303 Savage	190	S.P.	1,980	1,680	1,650	1,190	1.3	6.2	15.5
.300 H&H Magnum	180	Exp.	2,920	2,670	3,400	2,850	0.6	2.4	5.8
.300 H&H Magnum	220	Exp.	2,620	2,370	3,350	2,740	0.7	3.1	7.7
.303 British	215	S.P.	2,180	1,900	2,270	1,720	1.1	4.9	12.5
.32 Winchester Sp.	165	O.P.E.	2,280	1,920	1,900	1,350	1.0	4.7	12.5
.32 Winchester Sp.	170	S.P.	2,280	1,870	1,960	1,320	1.0	4.8	13.0
.32 Remington	170	S.P. & Exp.	2,220	1,890	1,860	1,350	1.0	4.9	13.0
.35 Remington	200	Exp.	2,210	1,830	2,170	1,490	1.1	5.2	14.0
.300 Winchester Mag.	150	S.P. & Exp.	3,400	3,050	3,850	3,100	0.4	1.9	4.8
.300 Winchester Mag.	180	S.P. & Exp.	3,070	2,850	3,770	3,250	0.5	2.1	5.3
.264 Win. Magnum	100	S.P.	3,700	3,260	3,040	2,360	0.4	1.6	4.2
.264 Win. Magnum	140	S.P.	3,200	2,940	3,180	2,690	0.5	2.1	4.9

S.P.—Soft Point   Exp.—Expanding   O.P.E.—Open Point Expanding

3 Evolution of the Deer Rifle

THE MODEL 94 Winchester carbine set the standard for today's deer rifle. It was the type of gun which appealed to the deer hunter, being light of weight for carrying and short for fast handling in the brush where most whitetails are hunted.

The Model 94 was originally introduced in 1894 and chambered for .32-40 and .38-55 black-powder cartridges. But it reached its peak of success when it was chambered for the popular .30/30 cartridge.

The first repeating rifles were heavy and cumbersome. They were not primarily hunting weapons; their foremost use was for protection. But the hunting of deer for food dates back to Plymouth Rock and thus each rifle was potentially a hunting weapon. But the emphasis on weight and fast-handling evolved well after the first repeating actions were perfected.

The first repeating rifle was the Volcanic, put into production in the late 1800's. It had a lever action and was the forerunner of the famous Winchester lever-action guns which revolutionized the concept of a deer-hunting weapon.

This revolutionary lever feed action of the Volcanic rifle was designed by B. Tyler Henry, and the gun was mass produced by what is now the Smith and Wesson Company. The Volcanic was followed by the Henry lever-action repeaters, and in 1866 the first rifle carrying the Winchester brand name was introduced—the Winchester '66 chambered for the .44-caliber rimfire cartridge. This particular rifle in different versions was in production for 25 years.

Winchester really came into its own, however, with the introduction of the Winchester '73—"The Gun that Won the West." This was a modification of the Winchester '66 and was chambered for the .44-40, first centerfire cartridge developed by Winchester. The cartridge had a .44-caliber bullet powered by a 40-grain powder charge.

Marlin introduced a lever-action repeater in 1881 for the .45-70 cartridge and also the .40-50-260 and the .45-85-285. The Marlin Firearms Company

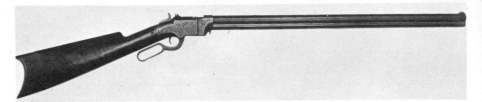

The first repeating rifle was the Volcanic, designed by B. Tyler Henry and put into production in the late 1880's. Its lever-action mechanism was the forerunner of the famous Winchester '66 and '73.

The Model 94 Winchester set the standard for today's deer rifle. Still a popular rifle, it is available in .30/30 and .32 Special.

Lightweight, economical Savage Model 342 in .30/30 is a fast-handling bolt-action rifle.

The Winchester Model 88, chambered for .308, .284 and .243, is a popular deer rifle. It weighs seven pounds and is hammerless.

The slide-action Remington Model 760 is one of the fastest-handling deer guns. It is chambered for the .270, .30/06, .35 Remington, .280 Remington and .308 Winchester.

earlier had brought out a single-shot lever gun in 1861 chambered for .32 long rimfire and centerfire cartridges.

Savage put its initial lever-action gun into production in 1895. It was made for Savage by the Marlin Firearms Company, and was chambered for the .303

cartridge. Savage's famous Model 99 was introduced in 1899, also chambered for the .303, and this has been a favorite deer-hunting weapon ever since. In 1912 the Model 99 was chambered for the .22 Savage Hi-Power, first rifle to take a high-powered .22-caliber cartridge, and in 1913 was first to be chambered for the .250-3000, the beginning of the low-trajectory loads of today. At the time, the 3000 feet-per-second velocity of the .250-3000 was almost unbelievable.

Soon thereafter, the bolt-action rifle was introduced, and coupled with the high-velocity cartridges, made an immediate hit. The autoloaders and pump-action rifles we know today are fairly recent innovations, coming into their own within the past couple of decades.

Nowadays the hunter can get a gun of his action choice in just about every deer-hunting cartridge imaginable. Bolt actions are preferred by the hunters seeking an "all-purpose" gun, to be used under a variety of conditions for a variety of game, from varmints to big game like deer. The reliable bolt action is also the most foolproof of all the actions. But strictly for deer hunting, the bolt never will be as popular as the lever, autoloader and pump because of the speed factor. The lever action is still far and away the most popular action among deer hunters. A rifle like the Marlin 336 chambered for the .35 Remington is lightweight and short enough for fast handling in dense timber, and the .35 Remington is a heavy bullet that ploughs through the brush. A combination such as this is ideal for the densely timbered deer woods of states such as Pennsylvania, New York and Virginia.

The most popular deer-hunting weapon nowadays still is the Model 94 Winchester, a position it never has relinquished, but other fairly recent introductions are making inroads into its sales.

Let's take a brief rundown of the more popular rifles available to the deer hunter today.

LEVER ACTION

Winchester Model 94—A solid frame hammer gun, 6-shot tubular magazine, 20-inch barrel, weight 6¼ pounds, chambered for .30/30 and .32 Special.

J. C. Higgins Model 45—6-shot full-length magazine, side ejection, hammer, 20-inch barrel, weight 6½ pounds, chambered for .30/30 and .35 Remington.

Winchester Model 88—Hammerless, 4-shot clip magazine, solid frame, short-stroke action, 22-inch barrel, weight 7 pounds, chambered for .308, .284 and .243. (Also .358, but this is not recommended for whitetail deer.)

Marlin Model 336—Hammer gun, carbine with 20-inch barrel, side ejection, 6-shot magazine, chambered for .30/30, .32 Special and .35 Remington.

Sako Finnwolf—A lever-action repeater made in Sweden. Hammerless. Weight 7 pounds, 24-inch barrel. Chambered for .243 and .308.

Savage Model 99F—Lightweight model with 24-inch barrel. Hammerless. Weight 6¾ pounds. 5-shot rotary magazine. Chambered for .300 Savage, .308 and .243.

AUTOLOADER

Ruger Carbine—Gas operated, 18½-inch barrel, 4-shot tubular magazine, weight 5¾ pounds, chambered for .44 Magnum cartridge.

Remington Model 742A—Gas operated, 22-inch barrel, 4-shot clip magazine, weight 7½ pounds, chambered for .30/06, .308, .280 and 6mm.

Winchester Model 100—Gas operated, 22-inch barrel, weight 7¼ pounds, 4-shot clip magazine, chambered for .243, .284 and .308.

PUMP

Remington Model 760A—Hammerless, 22-inch barrel (Model 760-ADL carbine has 18½-inch barrel), 4-shot clip magazine, weight 7½ pounds, chambered for .270, .30/06, .35 Remington, .280 Remington and .308 Winchester.

BOLT ACTION

Remington Model 600—Extremely short (37¼″) for fast handling. Monte Carlo stock. Weight 5½ pounds. Barrel length, 18½ inches. 5-shot capacity. Chambered for 6mm, .308, .35 Remington, and .222 Remington.

Browning Safari—Mauser action, 22-inch barrel. Weight 7 pounds. Rotary magazine. Chambered for .243, .264 Magnum, .270, .30/06 and .308.

Coltsman—Sako action, weight 6½ to 7½ pounds, chambered for .243, .264, .270, .308, .30/06 and .300 H&H Magnum.

Weatherby Mark V—Monte Carlo stock. Available in both right- and left-handed models. Weight about 7½ pounds. Chambered for .257 Weatherby Magnum, .270 WM, 7mm WM and .340 WM.

Sears & Roebuck Model 51L—HVA Swedish action, 22-inch barrel, weight 6½ pounds. 4-shot magazine, chambered for .243, .270, .30/06 and .308.

Remington Model 700—Weight 6¾ pounds. 20-inch barrel, 5-shot magazine. Chambered for .243, 6mm, .270, .280 Remington and .308.

Savage Model 340 Carbine—An economy-model rifle. Clip 3-shot magazine. 18½-inch barrel. Weight 6¼ pounds. Chambered for .30/30 and .222.

Savage Model 110—Weight 6¾ pounds, 22-inch barrel, 4-shot magazine. Chambered for .243, .270, .308 and .30/06. (Available in left-handed model.)

Winchester Model 70—Weight 7¾ pounds (about 6¾ pounds in featherweight model). 24-inch barrel (22 inches in featherweight). Chambered for .243, .270, .30/06, .308. 5-shot magazine.

4 Bullet Placement

HAVING A good rifle-sight combination doesn't necessarily make a hunter a better marksman. The rifle is just a precision tool. How well it functions depends on the man behind it. And knowing how to shoot properly is one of the glaring deficits among the modern-day hunting fraternity.

While researching this book, I talked to many people associated with deer hunters across the nation—outdoor writers, other hunters, conservation people —and almost to a man they voiced the same singular opinion: there just aren't many hunters who can shoot proficiently.

"Whatever happened to the hunter who knows what his rifle will do and can hit something with it?" said Richard Alden Knight, well-known outdoor columnist from Williamsport, Pennsylvania. "I know a few of them but they are in the minority. Yet, I still go deer hunting. I still show men how to dress out their first kill and how to track and finish off a cripple. I still look through the dark, cold woods for the incompetents. I do wish they would stay home."

Every hunter owes it to himself to be familiar with the sport of deer hunting before entering the woods; he should know his quarry and how to plan his strategy and tactics. And of course he should know how to handle a gun once game is sighted.

To learn to shoot a gun with some degree of success, the hunter has to practice. He must become familiar with his weapon, know what it will do under varied circumstances. This means shooting several boxes of ammunition through the gun.

Every hunter owes it to himself to take his favorite gun out of the closet prior to the season opener, wipe off the year's accumulation of dust, and fire it many times. In doing so he could well stack the odds of success in his favor. Many hunters spend painstaking days looking for a legal target, only to miss with their shot during that moment of truth when the sights are aligned and the hunter slowly sq-u-ee-z-es the trigger.

Confidence is all important in hunting. The shooter must have the utmost confidence in his weapon. Before he can practice with it and gain this needed confidence, he must know how it shoots, how accurate it is at different ranges. In other words, it must be sighted in properly.

Taking a gun out "cold" and trying to hunt with it is inviting trouble. It happened to me just last season and I'm still slightly red in the face. An editor of a well-known regional magazine contacted me about doing a test story for his publication on the Deerslayer .44 Magnum rifle. He said he would personally deliver the rifle to me. Could I line up a place for deer hunting?

I got in touch with a rancher friend of mine and he agreed to take us out the following Saturday. We were going to hunt on a spread where there were many antlerless deer permits available and the deer weren't spooky or wild. It was almost a dead cinch that we would get a reasonable shot at a deer.

Sure enough, we'd no sooner walked off into the pasture just after daybreak when a fat and sleek doe jumped from a knot of brush, ran out a few dozen yards and stopped, in the classic broadside pose. I was already fidgeting with my camera, reasoning the shot and kill were only routine procedure.

The gun boomed. Dust geysered over the doe's back. She leaped frantically and dashed out of sight over a small knoll. My editor friend shook his head dejectedly.

Five shots and five misses later, with three different deer as targets, I was becoming perturbed. I was sure the editor had target tested the gun and figured the misses were a result of his sloppy shooting ability.

Since I had one tag left on my hunting license, I told him to give me the rifle and I'd shoot him a deer for photos and a story. About an hour later I jumped a forkhorn buck that ran out about one hundred yards and stopped, half facing me. I centered the open sights behind the buck's shoulder and tightened my trigger finger.

The bullet spun the deer completely around. Imagine my surprise when he leaped to his feet and took off as if he'd never been touched. I ran to where the deer had been standing and searched for the telltale blood droppings. But there was nothing but a hat full of hair. Bobby Burnam, the rancher, examined the hair and said it had come off the deer's back. What had happened, he imagined, was that the bullet had grazed the deer along the back, giving it quite a shock but inflicting no permanent damage.

This had me puzzled. I'd aimed at the lower part of the body, yet the bullet sailed high. Could it be the sights? This prompted me to step off one hundred yards and shoot at a prickly pear cactus pad. The bullet kicked up dust a full twelve inches above the target. Other shots confirmed my suspicions. The rifle sights were far off.

The embarrassed editor admitted he'd never fired the gun. He'd unpacked it from the factory crate only the night before.

Suppose we'd jumped a trophy buck. Think how we would have regretted the oversight of not checking the rifle out properly. Yet it happens every day of the deer season, somewhere.

A hunter should sight in his own weapon and field test it regularly. Many nimrods simply turn their guns over to local gunsmiths and have them sight the weapons in. But there's always the possibility that the hunter and gun-smith don't see through the sights the same way.

Many years ago I was tied down with extra work just before the deer season opening, so I took a new rifle and scope I'd just acquired to a gunsmith friend of mine and asked him to check them out, sighting them in accurately. Afterwards he assured me the rifle was zeroed perfectly for one hundred yards.

The second day of the season I was pussyfooting along the side of a brushy header when I jumped a nice buck. He came from the brushy innards of the draw, turned abruptly and ran almost parallel to me, perhaps fifty yards away on the opposite side of the header. I couldn't have asked for an easier shot. I pulled down on the buck and missed him cleanly three successive times.

Back in camp at noon I was really bemoaning the muffed opportunity. My hunting companions asked if I'd checked out my rifle. No, I confessed, but a gunsmith had, and I was sure the fault didn't rest with the rifle. But just to be doubly sure, I laid off a makeshift range and fired a half-dozen test shots. Not a one was near the bull's-eye. I was shooting a good six inches high and to the right, at one o'clock on the target. A few adjustments on the scope and I was back in business again.

Sighting in a rifle is no complicated engineering feat. Anyone can do it by firing less than a box of ammo. It is only a matter of following a simple procedure.

I always sight in my rifles at twenty-five yards. This way, by figuring the trajectory of the bullet, I can pinpoint where it will be "on" again and how it will perform at different distances.

The trajectory of the bullet is the curve it follows in flight. A bullet doesn't travel in a straight line, but rather in a curve. By flatter trajectory is meant less curve of the bullet in flight.

At twenty-five yards the bullet will be striking the target the first time it crosses a horizonal plane. After this it will curve upwards, its mid-point tra-jectory being the farthest distance between the crest of the curve and the horizonal line. Then it will curve downward again, crossing the horizonal line again before dropping below it. When the lines bisect, this will be the point of impact again, the second spot where the rifle is "on." After this the bullet will drop, always shooting low in relation to the target.

By plotting the trajectory of your particular caliber rifle, you can determine the next point where the bullet will impact after the twenty-five yard mark. This will be about 175 yards for the .30/30. But at no place between the twenty-five yard mark and the second point where the curve and horizonal plane bisect, will the bullet be too far off the target. Certainly the aim will be more than adequate for deer hunting.

At the short range of twenty-five yards there is little doubt that the .first bullet fired will be on the paper target. But should it miss, you can get it on by bore sighting the rifle. Remove the bolt and steady the rifle on some kind of rest. Look through the bore until you have the target about centered. Then shift your gaze through the sight, adjusting it so the target is again about centered. This step only assures that you'll put a hole in the paper and will have some mark to work from.

From here the procedure is elementary. By changing the adjustments on your sights, you can move the bullet to hit where you desire.

On scope and peep (receiver) sights these adjustments come easy. But open sights are hard to change with any degree of accuracy. This is still another reason why either the scope or peep is the preference over open sights.

The scope and peep both have adjustments that are graduated in minutes of angle, or fractions thereof. A minute of angle means a movement of the bullet one inch at one hundred yards. Therefore, if you were shooting four inches to the right at one hundred yards, you'd want to move your line of sight four minutes of angle to the left. Most receiver and scope sights have two adjustments, one for elevation and one for windage, or horizonal.

Since the minute of angle means one inch of movement at one hundred yards, then it stands to reason that it will move the bullet only one-quarter of an inch at twenty-five yards. So if you wish to compensate for four inches at twenty-five yards, you'd move the adjustment dial sixteen clicks, assuming each click represented one minute of angle.

With open sights there is a crude notched bar for elevation adjustment, but to compensate for windage the hunter must move either the rear or front sight by tapping it over in its grooved seat. The rear sight is moved in the direction the shooter wants to shift his bullet. If he is shooting high, then he moves the rear sight higher. The front sight, however, is moved in the opposite direction. Should the bullet be striking to the left, he'd change the front sight to the right, or the back sight to the left. There are no windage adjustments at all and moving the bullet by sliding the sight in its groove is simply a matter of trial and error.

After the rifle is zeroed in at twenty-five yards, it is best to check it out at a longer distance. One hundred yards is a likely choice. Any mistakes at twenty-five yards will be multiplied four times at the longer distance. At this range the rifle should be shooting a little high, as the curve of the trajectory has not bisected the horizonal line for the second time. But with reference to windage it should be in the center of the target.

After you have your rifle sighted in and you are all checked out on its operation, you are ready to go hunting. One of the most impressive things you learn in the hunting woods is that there is a marked difference between shooting at an inanimate target and live game.

The foremost tendency among shooters is to aim for the largest part of the deer. This is the mid-section. Actually, it is the very worst place you could place your bullet. A paunch-hit deer may run miles without falling, and may leave very little blood to follow.

Deer have several vulnerable areas where a well-placed bullet will bring instant death. The three most popular are behind the shoulder, the neck and the heart.

Probably the most logical thing to aim for is what is commonly referred to as the "high lung shot." This is just behind the shoulder, about 40 per cent of the way down the body below the spine. Here the hunter has the greatest margin for error. If he is shooting either high or low, he'll still place his bullet in vital regions. A low shot will hit in the vicinity of the heart; a high bullet will penetrate around the spine. Forward the bullet will shatter the shoulders, a little way back it will strike high in the paunch, which is much more deadly than a low paunch hit.

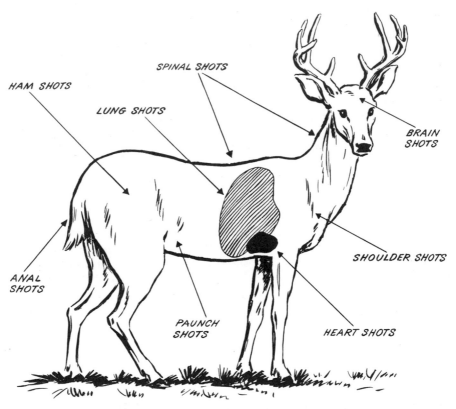

The deer's most vulnurable areas are behind the shoulder in the lungs, the neck and the heart. Neck and heart shots are difficult to make, though, so the hunter's best bet is a well-placed lung shot. Avoid paunch shots, if possible; a deer hit there often will run miles before falling.

Many veteran hunters aim for the neck. A deer struck in the neck with a high-powered rifle seldom will run far. And in this region there is a minimum loss of edible meat. But the neck of the whitetail deer is very small and there isn't much margin for error. A bullet placed either slightly high or low will be a miss.

The heart of the deer is carried much lower in the body cavity than most people realize. The very location of the blood-pumping organ makes it hard to reach with a bullet without destroying excessive meat, save for the flat broadside shot. The heart, most vital organ in the animal, is well protected with muscles and tissue. Any shot angled into this region is naturally going to mess up lots of choice eating venison.

And speaking of angles, this is something which every hunter should take into consideration. Seldom will a deer take a statue pose, still and broadside. Chances are much better that it will be moving away or standing at an angle. The hunter must mentally plot the path of the bullet to keep from completely ruining the animal for eating purposes.

Once I was sitting in a tree stand in central Texas, watching a long, open avenue which quartered off through the cedar brush. After a long wait of several hours an eight-point buck came slipping down the game trail. I was impatient after the wait and I didn't give the deer time to get out into the open, where I would have a clear shot. Instead, I tried to shoot over a small bush and angle a bullet into the buck's spine. When shooting from an elevated position, the tendency is to overshoot. I didn't compensate for this. The bullet passed over the spine and nicked the deer's left shoulder blade. All I succeeded in doing was crippling the animal, something no conscientious hunter wants to do.

This composite picture of angles is another reason why the behind-the-shoulder shot is the best and most logical choice. Here the hunter has more leeway. Should the deer be running away at a tangent, a bullet placed behind the shoulder will angle forward, exiting just in front of the opposite shoulder, a surefire killing blow. From above, the bullet will angle down, through the chest cavity, also a vulnerable area. Entering from the front it will angle back through the innards, or from below it will pass upwards around the spine. Any of these shots will do the job.

When a deer is presenting itself at an angle, always think in terms of the shoulder bone structure. This is above the bottom of the body about a quarter of the way up, away from the foreleg bone. Any bullet placed around the shoulders this high is a good shot in a vulnerable area.

Probably the two most difficult shots are when the deer is either directly facing the shooter or is facing straight away. A deer in either of these poses doesn't offer much of a target. A running deer coming head-on or going directly away is particularly difficult to hit since the small target area is bouncing erratically. Even when the deer is motionless there is only a tiny area to shoot at.

When a deer is facing head-on, aim for the spot where the neck merges with the body. A bullet placed here will expand in the chest, causing much damage. If you can only see the deer's rear, put the bullet at the base of the tail, driving the projectile into the body cavity, ultimately into the chest.

In shooting deer, placing the bullet is of utmost importance. It can't do its intended job unless it strikes vital organs. A correctly placed bullet should do one of two things: disrupt the nervous system, such as in the brain or spine, or stop vital life processes like the heart or lungs. A gut or belly shot is the worst of all. It eventually will bring death, but the deer usually will run a long way before dropping, and it often leaves an indiscernible blood trail.

Second to bullet placement is bullet action. I once saw a deer almost escape after being shot with a handloaded cartridge meant for target shooting. It ran for about 300 yards before we were fortunate enough to find it. The exit hole of the bullet was about the same size as the entrance hole. Since a bullet kills primarily by shock, this slug by failing to expand or mushroom, was robbed of most of its effectiveness.

It is for this reason that I prefer a high-velocity cartridge like the 100-grain bullet in .243 (3,070 fps muzzle velocity) or 150-grain .30/06 bullet (2,970 fps) to the .35 Remington (2,210 fps with the 200-grain bullet) and the .30/30 (2,220 fps with the 170-grain bullet). If the terrain permits, I always go to the fast-moving bullets because of their shocking power. The whitetail deer probably is the most thin-skinned of all big-game animals. Not a whole lot of bullet penetration is necessary. Any big-game cartridge is going to get inside and do damage, rather than exploding upon impact with the skin.

A slower traveling bullet like the .35 Remington sort of ploughs through the deer. The .243, on the other hand, hits with such devastating speed that any tissue will offer enough resistance to mushroom the bullet, creating tremendous shock waves. With the heavier bullets which leave the rifle muzzles at speeds between 2,200 fps and 2,500, I prefer soft-point bullets which tend to spread out rather than to force their way through tissue doing little damage. Some cartridges designed for bigger game, where the accent is more on penetration, are not too satisfactory for whitetail deer. This is particularly true of bullets in the 200-grain class. The modern deer cartridge, like the 100-grain Winchester Silvertip for the .243, is designed with both penetration and expanding ability considered. There is just enough outside protection on the bullet to get it through the skin, in where it is supposed to do its damage.

What this boils down to is that the deer's vitals are on the inside, not the outside. A bullet which passes through the largest segment of the body in the upper part, around the chest, is going to do the most damage. A shot that ruins less meat and still brings instant death is the perfect shot, but whenever there is doubt, shoot for a kill, toward the forequarters. Best to have a dead deer on the ground with a sizable chunk of damaged venison than a crippled one off somewhere in the woods.

5 Care of the Deer Rifle

THE MODERN deer rifle is a precision tool that never will wear out in a hunter's lifetime with normal usage. There is an old axiom that the rifle is only as good as the man behind it. Equally true, the rifle is only as good as the care it receives. Many rifle malfunctions have occurred at that moment of truth when the hunter puts the sights on a deer and squeezes the trigger simply because the gun hasn't been cared for properly.

Whenever the hunter comes in from the field, he should immediately run over his rifle with an oily rag or a silicone-impregnated cloth, available from any sporting goods store. Also good is spray oil. Packaged under pressure, a slight push of a button will spray a fine mist of oil over the gun and into the action, protecting it against the elements. In the deer camp the hunter should always take a few moments to accomplish this preventive maintenance. Once he returns home he can give the rifle a more thorough cleaning before he puts it away.

Preventing rust is the most important consideration when caring for a gun. Unprotected steel, unless it is the stainless variety, rusts when exposed to air which contains oxygen and moisture. Acids, salts and other corrosive substances, when touched to metal by some means or other, start a reaction that soon leaves the exposed surface layered with rust.

Cleaning a gun is no longer an arduous task as it was in pioneer days when cleaning materials were crude—hot water, ramrod, cloth and hog fat. The smoking black powder left the bore in a mess and sometimes it required hours to completely clear the smudge out. The general procedure back in the days of my grandfather's youth was to pour boiling water through the barrel, continuously swabbing the bore with a cloth at the same time. The water had to be boiling so the non-stainless bore would dry instantly, and when the water ran out clean, the gun was ready to be heavily coated with hog fat.

Today, thanks to modern rust-resisting chemicals, the job requires only a few minutes. But this time factor shouldn't subtract from the importance of keeping a deer rifle in tiptop shape.

After every hunting trip, the deer rifle should be thoroughly cleaned. A kit containing a cleaning rod, light oil, grease, patches, solvent and brass brushes is an essential part of the hunter's equipment.

If a hunter has been handling his gun with sweaty hands and it has been exposed to open air, the metal already has begun to rust once it is allowed to stand for a few hours. This is why it is imperative that the gun is cleaned thoroughly before being stored away. And one note of caution. Care should be taken before storing a gun in a sheepskin-lined case. Such a case which zippers shut captures moisture inside. As the air inside the case warms, there is a condensation of moisture which invades the moving parts of the gun's action, causing rust.

It isn't difficult to remove rust once it has taken hold if caught in time. Light rust can be removed with fine steel wool without usually leaving any visible signs. If the steel wool leaves marks, they should be retouched with a bluing substance.

After excessive shooting, flecks of lead often show up in the rifle's bore. Unless this lead is removed it may impair the accuracy of your firearm. It most times can be successfully scrubbed out with a brass brush, available in the proper caliber size at any sporting goods store. The brushes should be free of dirt and lint. I have found it best to store them individually in plastic boxes. Those cylindrical tubes which prescriptions come in make dandy containers.

Sometimes, however, the lead must be removed chemically. Any chemical containing a large percentage of mercury will do as long as the other ingredients will not harm metal. One of the best removers is Blue Ointment, which is about one-third mercury, and is available at most drugstores. Coat the bore heavily with ointment and leave it overnight. The mercury and lead will form an amalgam which is easily wiped out. In some cases the procedure may have to be repeated several times.

Easiest way to obtain complete materials for gun cleaning is to buy one of the ready-made kits found in any sporting goods store. A kit includes everything for a complete cleaning job and usually the ingredients are packed in a sturdy container. It contains a cleaning rod, a light oil, grease, cleaning patches, solvent and brass brushes. Usually the kits are packaged for individual calibers.

It always is best to examine the ingredients of such kits before purchasing one. Get nothing but the best materials, for any hunter is no better than the weapon he packs. Sometimes you may prefer to purchase each item separately and make up a kit of your own.

A good cleaning rod is a necessity. Metal ones are far superior to wood and brass. Many good ones are on the market, both solid and jointed. The jointed ones are much more compact and usually are quite durable. The better ones also have two or three interchangeable tips and a revolving handle.

Cotton flannel makes good cleaning patches. Flannel is tough and won't tear as easily as most other fabrics. Most commercial patches are made from flannel. A patch should be roughly two inches square.

An old toothbrush is a handy item in a kit, to be used in reaching tight places inside the gun's chamber and action.

Any of the better-known oils and greases are good. I prefer 3-in-1 Oil and Gunslick, although there are many others just as acceptable. So that none of the items will be lost, it is best to store all of them together in a sturdy, compact box.

Cleaning a rifle is a simple procedure. First swab the bore thoroughly with a solvent such as Hoppe's No. 9, then push through three or four clean patches to dry the bore. Follow with a thin coating of grease. Rub the outside down thoroughly and cover with a thin layer of oil.

Most people overuse the oil. Too much oil harms the stock and runs down into the action. An old cartridge case inserted into the breech serves as good protection against chemicals and grease finding their way from the bore into the firing mechanism. It also is advisable to store guns muzzle down so that excess oil will drain away from the action.

Firing mechanisms often have too much oil rather than too little. In excessive cold temperatures too much oil may congeal, causing the gun to malfunction. Oil should be applied to the mechanism by the drop, and only one drop to each part which requires a lubricant, or spray a fine mist over the parts with a pressurized can. Finely powdered graphite is a good lubricant that won't congeal in cold weather and it can be obtained in most five-and-ten stores.

Caution is the keynote when cleaning a telescopic sight. A scope lens has a delicate coated surface which is easily scratched. A specially treated cloth used for cleaning ordinary eyeglasses is good for scope lenses and will keep them from fogging. The next best is photographic lens tissue. A substitute in the field is a badly worn bill of currency. Never use handkerchiefs or other rough cloths for they tend to scratch lenses. Also be cautious when applying oil to the outside of the scope and don't get any on the lenses. Frequently, it pays to check the scope screws to make sure they are tight and the scope is sturdily mounted.

With open or peep sights, ordinary match smoke will help reduce glare.

The front blade sight should be checked from time to time to see if it has been knocked loose. Also a spot check will assure that the back sight is seated on the correct elevation notch.

The luster on dull stocks can be restored by rubbing linseed oil into the wood. Several applications may be necessary to get the finish exactly as you want it. Any of the bluing chemicals found in sporting goods stores are good for covering small worn parts on the metal. A full-scale bluing job takes much equipment and is a gunsmith's job.

A pre-hunt check of the rifle's safety is a simple precaution that no hunter should overlook.

6 Equipment

ONE OF the really appealing aspects of deer hunting is that no elaborate equipment is needed. Theoretically, a person probably could get by on what he's got in the closet at home, excepting his weapon. Of course, there are certain refinements which make the sport more attractive and productive.

Take binoculars, for example. Many hunters have a misconception that binoculars are designed for long-distance work, in the wide-open spaces. Since most whitetails are killed at a range of seventy-five yards or less, binoculars often are overlooked as a deer-hunting asset.

In the brushy habitat of the whitetail deer, binoculars can perform a specific job. A pair with good light-gathering capabilities can aid in probing the dark areas where deer can stand quietly and remain undetected. The hunter sitting still and looking often can see much more than when on the move. Sometimes just a flick of the ear or movement of the tail will give the deer away. By probing the brush with binoculars the hunter might detect this telltale movement when otherwise he would overlook it.

A scope sight will not substitute for binoculars, despite what you may have heard. The twin-eye picture of binoculars gives more field of view and depth perception. The scope sight was designed to aim through, nothing more. Binoculars accomplish the job of detecting deer much more effectively.

A standard pair of binoculars generally will have two numbers stamped somewhere on it, such as 6x30. The first number designates the power of the glass. Six would mean six power, or six times the magnification. An animal 600 yards away would be seen through the binoculars the size it would appear at one hundred yards to the naked eye. The second number, in this instance thirty, is the diameter in millimeters of the objective lens, the large one farthest from your eye.

Divide the first number into the second and you get the light-gathering potential of the instrument, or the exit pupil as it is called. For the 6x30 binoculars, the exit pupil would be 5mm. A 7x35 glass would also have an exit pupil of 5 mm, a 7x50 one of 7mm, and so forth. The higher the last number the heavier the binoculars, since the objective lens will be larger and will require a larger housing.

Since the eye won't dilate to more than 5mm under any normal hunting situation, a glass with a larger exit pupil won't be fully utilized. Personally, I prefer a light instrument when deer hunting, one that won't cause the strap to dig into the muscles of my neck. Something in the 6x30 or 7x35 class is more than adequate for whitetail deer terrain.

Notice that neither of the numbers has anything to do with field of view. This designation is stamped on only a few of the better quality binoculars. It may be shown in numbers like 435′, which is the field of view in feet at 1000 yards, or it may be in degrees, such as 7°. Using the formula of one degree field of view equals 521⁄2 feet at 1000 yards, you can determine the field of view for your particular instrument. The lower the power of the binoculars, the more field of view it will have.

The wider field of view is desirable in whitetail hunting since it will aid in studying areas of cover more extensively. In this kind of hunting the human is searching for some specific part of the animal, rather than using the instrument to sweep across a vast swath of landscape simply looking for game. Often binoculars will reveal slight twitches of movement that will give the deer away, movement which would go undetected by the naked eye. It also helps immeasurably when searching for the telltale antlers of a deer standing half-hidden in the shadows.

Hunting clothes will vary with the locale. The deer hunter in Minnesota naturally would require different clothing than would the Texas hunter. But there are some basics to remember when shopping for hunting togs.

Underwear is very important. The hunter with a good foundation will remain warm and comfortable while the hunter with inadequate underwear will not. It is that simple.

The newer insulated thermal-action underwear has taken much of the drudgery out of deer hunting. The hunter of today can remain warmer while wearing less. I prefer the two-piece underwear since the top can be removed or left off during warmer days. Insulated underwear works on the theory of capturing air between garment and skin to keep the hunter warm. It is much more effective and comfortable than the old cotton and wool longjohns.

Wool is still the most popular material for outer garments. Because of its porosity, wool provides warmth on the coldest days, yet is still fairly cool on warm fall days. The shirt should be in a red, bright yellow or flame orange color for safety precautions.

In trousers wool and canvas are the two time-honored favorites, but khaki and denim are also popular. I still like bluejeans, which stand up nicely against the punishment trousers take in the brush. The hunter can choose either the straight-leg pants or those which taper at the ankles, to fit snugly inside hunting boots.

Jackets come in varied materials, from wool and canvas and khaki to the newer synthetics like nylon, Dacron and Acrilan. The old popular standby canvas probably stands up best for brush wear, and the better ones are waterproofed. The jacket, like the shirt, should be in some vivid color like red, yellow or orange.

Probably the most important of all the hunter's apparel is the footgear. There is nothing more miserable than trying to sit statue-still on a deer stand while your feet are aching from cold. Socks, as well as the boots, are all important. Wool is good because the material cushions the feet and keeps them warm, but I like the newer insulated socks even better. A single pair of lightweight insulated socks will keep the feet warm during even the most severe weather.

When buying boots always get them large enough to take the heavier socks. A good hunting boot should be waterproof. I like a spongy rubber sole since it makes for easier walking, especially on rocky soil, and it is quieter. Some of the newer all-rubber boots are comfortable, quiet, waterproof and warm. The height of the boot depends on personal preference.

In the way of a cap, get one large enough so the ear flaps give adequate protection. A good hunting cap also should be waterproof, and in a brilliant color for safety.

Gloves are optional. Personally, I find it difficult to handle a rifle adequately while wearing gloves, but some of my friends wear them without any apparent disadvantage. One man I know cuts the trigger finger from his glove so he can readily get his finger inside the trigger guard without hindrance.

Clothing can make a hunting trip successful or a curse. The hunter who is miserable in the field won't enjoy his sport, and his chances of bagging game are much reduced.

Other than this, little equipment is actually needed. If you're planning on straying away from the road a good ways, always have a compass in your pocket and know how to use it. Another asset is a waterproof box of matches.

Some sort of knife is needed to dress the kill. Most hunters like the common hunting knife, carried on a belt sheath which rests on the hip. Personally, I lean to a pocketknife with a four-inch blade, because it seems my hunting knife is continually hanging on brush and deals me misery when I'm sitting on a deer stand. Again, this is simply a matter of personal choice, but remember that a big knife isn't needed to dress a deer. One with a four-inch blade is more than adequate.

I always wear a wristwatch when deer hunting. It serves several useful purposes. For one, it aids me in keeping appointments, when I'm with other hunters. It also makes me more tolerant on a deer stand. Without this guide, I'm always inclined to move too soon. A watch forces me to be more patient and tenacious.

A rifle sling also comes in handy at times. Not an elaborate shooting sling, understand, just an ordinary carrying sling. A shooting sling is designed to steady the rifle for long-range shooting. Obviously you don't need that in deer hunting, at least not in most places where the whitetail roams. A carrying sling is nothing more than a strap of leather which fits on the swivels which come on many big-game rifles. A few temporary slings don't even call for the swivels; they snap on around the stock and rifle barrel. The sling allows you to throw the rifle over your shoulder, out of your hands when packing in a deer or maybe climbing into a tree stand.

A hand warmer is particularly helpful to the stand hunter in cold climes. The stalk hunter at least gets to move about, keeping his blood circulating. A stocking-type face protector, one that slips over the head with holes for the eyes, nose and mouth, also is comfortable. A hooded poncho that falls loosely around the body and is durable enough not to tear in the brushy habitat of the whitetail, is best for rainy weather.

A short length of rope is nice to have along when hanging up a dressed deer to keep it away from dirt and insects. Rope is also needed for tying the deer's feet together so a pole can be inserted for two hunters to pack the animal out. A sturdy plastic bag will carry the heart and liver of the deer, keeping fresh blood off your body and clothing. Another asset is a compact light-mesh deer bag, which fits over the deer and protects it from flies and other insects.

Remember, every piece of equipment you carry should be functional. Don't carry an item just because you feel you *might* need it. The hunter who travels light will travel comfortably. And in the deer woods there is no substitute for comfort.

7 Stand Hunting

THERE IS one basic trait of deer behavior that every hunter should keep in mind: a deer's eyes are conditioned to movement and it can be fooled by something which does not move.

The hunter who sits still, letting the deer move about and make the mistakes, is going to have much more success than the one who tries to carry the play to the sly creatures. The stand hunter not only is going to see more game, he's also going to get better shots. This is particularly true in areas where there are a lot of hunters moving about, keeping the deer scattered. In most circumstances, the stand hunter is going to get a shot at standing or slow-moving game, when moving around he might have to take a snap shot at one on the run. An immobile target naturally is going to be easier to hit and there's more chance for putting the bullet into a vital area.

Take a locale like the Catskill Mountains near Hunter, New York. Here every hotel has a prominent sign out front proclaiming "Welcome Hunters." And in they flock, by the thousands. Come opening day of the season and you'll see the flash of red and yellow shirts everywhere in the trees. This army of aimlessly wandering hunters is going to keep the deer on the move, and the man who picks a likely spot, on a good deer run, and waits patiently is the man who is most apt to bring home the venison.

Deer trails, or so-called "runs," are used year after year, generation after generation. But deer will change their habits with the seasons, as the food sources change. One month they may be feeding predominately on wild fruit; the next month on acorns. A trail may appear worn and well traveled, yet the evidence might be from the past. The idea, of course, is to locate a trail that is in use, or better yet, a spot where several trails come together.

But a hunter doesn't simply wander into the woods and come to a likely spot by chance. There is too much country to cover. The wise hunter has a plan, a pattern he will follow. He knows the terrain and he knows the best spots to pinpoint his insidious ambush.

47

I can't emphasize too strongly the need for becoming familiar with the country you are to hunt. Take a day prior to the season and just walk leisurely through the woods, looking for deer sign and prominent landmarks. This serves a twofold purpose. It helps you locate your stands in the most strategic places and it might prevent you from becoming lost while hunting, when your mind is intent on something else.

I like to get out about two days after a rain. This way all the tracks I find will be fresh. They'll readily stand out in the moist turf. Search along the worn avenues through the timber. Just a glance will ascertain whether or not deer are currently using the trail. Particularly good are trails leading into patches of dense cover, where deer likely will bed down. This way, if you are on stand at daybreak, you can intercept any animal traveling from its feeding area to its bedding ground. Also good are trails leading to salt and mineral licks, where deer have been lapping on rocks to obtain necessities of their diet.

After finding a trail that deer are traveling you can then situate your stand. If you're at ground level, wait at a spot where you can see as much country as possible. If the area isn't too open, at least be where you can see through the underbrush, watching for the legs of a moving animal. Also situate your stand where the existing or prevailing wind won't blow your scent into the path of the oncoming deer.

Many persons have the misconception that stand hunting requires no special ability. Nothing could be further from the truth. Successful stand hunting is a true art, fully as demanding as other forms of hunting. One hunter might see numerous deer pass his stand; another a scant hundred yards away might not see anything.

The hunter can't haphazardly wander into the woods, idly search out a

The stand-hunter should pick a spot near trails used by deer in their travels for food, water, and dense cover for bedding-down. Then he should get as comfortable as possible—and remain absolutely motionless.

stand, sit down and expect deer to start blundering over him. Position of the stand is vitally important. And there are other considerations, too.

The foremost consideration, of course, is to be hunting in known deer habitat. With any hunting, locating the game is half the solution to the mystery. The hunter in an area with an abundant population of deer is improving his chances tenfold for success.

Deer must have two basic things to survive, food and water. Protection also is important, but not nearly as much as the above mentioned two. Deer feed on such varied plants in various parts of the country that it would be impossible to chronicle them all here. The hunter seeking a prospective area to pursue his favorite sport should make local inquiries as to the best spots to hunt.

Once you have a general area pinpointed, look through it for more concrete deer signs, like tracks, droppings, browsed bushes and telltale trails . of travel. Try to situate your stand in an area where signs indicate a good concentration of deer. Locate it so that you command a view of a good deer run. Deer follow regular routes and these "runs" can be distinguished where the grass is worn away, evidence of travel.

Some hunters have the misconception that they must get as far away from camp as possible to hunt. True, in many instances it pays to get off the beaten path, back in the wilderness where there are fewer hunters. But in areas where there is less competition a stand a few hundred yards from camp might be as effective as one mile away.

An acquaintance of mine was telling about a hunt he made a few years ago in Jefferson National Forest, located in the mountainous part of western Virginia. On opening day of the season he slipped out of camp just at daybreak and walked for perhaps 500 yards when he came to a good deer run. Evidence showed that deer had been traveling frequently along this trail. Playing a hunch, the hunter found a good comfortable spot beside a tree, hunkered down, leaned back and prepared for a long wait. But less than thirty minutes later a nice buck came tiptoeing down the trail and one shot put him down. It was a simple feat to drag the deer back to camp. The hunter had been gone less than an hour.

It isn't always that easy, of course, but you can never tell about deer hunting. One of the biggest bucks I ever saw killed in New Mexico was slain by a hunter sitting in camp. He was busy cleaning his rifle when he chanced to glance up and there stood this handsome buck in a clearing less than one hundred yards away. The man gingerly fed a cartridge into the chamber, raised the rifle and bowled the deer over.

Tom McNally, distinguished outdoor editor of the Chicago *Tribune* and a world-renowned hunter, will tell you that stand hunting pays off—and he has one of the biggest bucks ever killed in Illinois to prove it. This one was bagged several years ago during a controlled hunt on the Horseshoe Lake Waterfowl Refuge near Cairo, at the southern end of the state.

McNally recalls that he'd found himself a likely spot in the swampy country to watch all about him. From his vantage point on a rotting log he could see clearly sixty yards in any direction through the cedars and oaks.

He had been sitting statue-like for maybe two hours, watching and listening, when suddenly he saw an immense buck step from the brush. The deer was perhaps ninety yards away—too far for a shot with the 20-gauge shotgun loaded with rifled slugs that McNally carried—and was angling across the swamp. McNally remembers that, at the time, he eased off the log and crouched behind it, hopeful the deer, a monster of a buck with antlers like those of an elk, might come closer, but afraid it would walk right on by him.

Suddenly on the other side of the deer a shotgun boomed. The buck immediately swerved and came right at McNally, in a fast trot. Tom rested his shotgun over the log and waited until the deer passed into a clearing. Quickly he shot—once, twice. The deer sagged to his knees, then fell heavily.

This one had a 23⅞-inch antler spread, sported 14 points and field-dressed 212 pounds.

The hunter who has a predetermined site for his stand has much better odds of scoring than does the person who tries to locate a likely stand the same day he plans to hunt. A stand should command a view of as much terrain as possible. In some areas this might be several hundred yards; in the brush it may be limited to seventy-five feet or less.

There are basically two types of stands, ground level and elevated. A ground-level stand may be nothing more than the hunter leaning up against a tree, or maybe he'll construct a sort of enclosure of branches and brush for concealment. In areas where they are legal, tree stands are popular. By climbing into the fork of a tree, the hunter has a wider view of terrain, he's up where deer seldom look, and any breeze tends to blow his scent high and away, rather than along the ground where deer can detect it.

In Florida, a hunter will pick a tree and erect a platform in it, sometimes

A tree stand allows the hunter to remove himself from the deer's natural direction of sight. Also, any scent he may leave will be blown high and away rather than along the ground where the deer can detect it.

an elaborate one; often nothing more than a board nailed in a fork. It is considered the lowest form of sportsmanship to get in another man's tree stand. In fact, it is almost sacrilegious.

A prominent landmark in southern Texas is a windmill-like structure, a high tripod contraption, standing forlornly in the brush. Here, where, incidentally, all hunting is done on private lands, the artificial stands are erected to allow the hunter to get up high where he can look down in the patches of clearing scattered through the chest-high spiny brush. There are no trees here to speak of, certainly none high enough to climb into for a stand.

When you approach your stand, do so from upwind. Get right in and settle down, avoiding as much unnecessary moving around as possible since this leaves your offensive odor spread everywhere. A deer's nose is its primary protection and this whiff of human odor is one danger signal no creature of the wild ignores. And we want to stress again: put any prevailing wind into your face, or blowing in at a tangent, not to your back where your scent will be carried into the area you're watching.

Once on the stand, you must possess, above all things, patience and confidence and endurance. You might be tied to that spot for a long, uncomfortable wait. But at all times you must take the positive approach, confident that the next minute may be the magic time when that long-awaited deer walks into view. A man needs this self-confidence to hunt off a stand properly.

To have tenacity, the hunter must be comfortable. This means getting a stand where you can sit naturally and comfortably. Cramped muscles are the bugaboo of every stand hunter. Every time he moves for relief he is making movement and noise that an alert deer might pick up.

Wear warm, comfortable clothing. It is better to be overdressed than underdressed. A chilled hunter is a careless hunter. Since much of the cold

On some private lands artificial blinds are constructed on steel tripods. Such a stand protects hunters from unpleasant weather and is high enough to provide a good vantage point for observation.

originates from the ground, take along something like a piece of tarp or heavy plastic to sit on. Also carry something to eat and a canteen of water. Don't try to push yourself unnecessarily. You're only defeating your basic purpose.

Many people can't adapt to stand hunting. They simply don't have the patience. It is difficult to do a complete changeabout, from the hustle and bustle of everyday life to simply waiting quietly, making like a statue. Ten minutes after the nervous hunter sits down he starts fighting the urge to move. He must brush at his nose or scratch his arm or sneeze or clear his throat—all giveaway sounds to the probing eyes and ears of a nearby deer.

Just remember that the stand hunter's basic strategy is remaining absolutely motionless. If the human is moving, even when he's got terrain and wind in his favor, it is increasingly difficult to slip up on a wary, alert deer. You are challenging the animal in its own bailiwick. But when you are sitting still, it is the animal that is moving about, making the mistakes. In stand hunting you are playing the odds.

Guy Clymer, a rancher friend of mine who has observed deer and their habits for more than forty years, said one of the animals won't pay much attention to a man out in the open, in the most conspicuous clothing, if he remains perfectly still. Yet sudden, abrupt movement is what gives the

This whitetail buck walked within range of the hunter waiting silently at his stand. Patience and the ability to sit absolutely still are the key to successful stand hunting.

hunter away. A deer might not be overly alarmed by a slow, easy movement of an arm or leg, yet that flick of fast, unnatural movement may send a wily old buck pounding off into the brush.

Rather than fidgeting a little all the time, it is much better to sit absolutely still for as long as you can stand it, then move everything at once. Every couple of hours, or however long you can endure the motionless wait, get up, stomp your feet, wiggle your arms to get the circulation going again, smoke a cigarette. Do this for a few minutes, then settle back down for another long drawn-out endurance run. Perhaps it will be days before you even spot a legal deer. It is frustrating at times, but often very rewarding.

A hunter who bagged one of the biggest bucks ever to come from the Black Hills region of South Dakota learned the value of stand hunting quite accidentally. It happened four, maybe five years ago. The hunter and his companion had separated and gone different ways into the densely wooded hills, in an area below Rapid City. All day they stalked through the draws and along the ridges covered heavily with pines and oaks without seeing a buck. Finally, just before sundown, the first hunter came to an old logging road where he'd agreed to meet his companion. He sat down on the thick carpet of fallen leaves, rested his back against a large pine tree and waited, watching down the road for some sign of his companion. But instead, about

Using a tree stump to break his outline, a hunter waits silently for an approaching deer. Keep the wind at your face so your scent is carried away from the area you are observing. *Courtesy U.S. Forest Service*

ten minutes later, two deer came into view around a bend, walking leisurely up the road. The lead one was a doe, but behind her came this massive buck. There really was no time to get excited. The hunter threw up his rifle and put a .30/06 slug in the buck's brisket.

Who knows, the same could happen to you. That very next minute may be the climax to the long and muscle-cramping hours you've spent waiting and watching and listening. That's why it always pays to remain alert.

Those hours of waiting are amply rewarded when that magic moment arrives—a handsome buck walks into your sights and tumbles to the ground.

8 Stalking and Tracking

THE GREATEST challenge in hunting is getting out and meeting the whitetail deer on its own terms in its own bailiwick. Stalking, it is called. The hunter pussyfoots stealthily through the woods, always watching and listening. Being constantly on the move, he naturally looks at more hunting territory than he would stand hunting. But at the same time, he's making himself more open to detection.

The hunter *can* sneak up on deer. I've done it numerous times. It only requires a special technique with accent on speed. Slow speed, that is. The slower the better.

I recall a buck I fooled this way two seasons back. I was hunting in west-central Texas, in Kimble County near the town of Junction, in wild and rugged country of canyons and deep-cut draws, liberally sprinkled with rocks. It was the type of country where a hunter must be doubly cautious to keep from announcing his approach to every deer within hundred of yards.

All day I was continually on the move. Once that morning, a wise old buck outwitted me. There was an oval-shaped flat, studded with mesquite trees, fanning out in front of a sharp-rising hill. The deer had bedded down on the side of the hill where he could watch the flat and glimpse anything that suggested danger.

I was still a full 200 yards from the hill when I spotted movement up near the hog-back ridge. I got my scope sight on it just as the fleeing deer topped the rise and vanished down the other side. As the deer crossed over I got a glimpse of antlers, a bragging-sized rack of antlers. This deer didn't live to enjoy old age by being dumb.

But actually, a deer isn't smart. At least not in the way we reckon smartness and intelligence. It is cunning and sly, all right, but not smart with the facility of gathering facts and reasoning a situation out.

The hunter can think. This is his one big advantage. If he knows deer habitat and the kind of terrain the critters prefer, he can, by simple deduc-

It takes great skill and stamina to stalk a deer within rifle range. *Courtesy Sask. Govt.*

tion, know where to plan his stalk in order to assure the greatest odds for success.

Later that same day, near sundown, I'd dropped over a knoll and into a basin-like depression filled with persimmon trees and small cedar bushes. It was a likely looking spot for deer, so I slowed up and really started concentrating and looking, taking each step as if I were walking on egg shells. I skirted a clump of brush and walked right up on a feeding deer. It was half-hidden behind a squat cedar, but when it heard me it threw up its head, above the bush.

The first thing I noticed was antlers. I threw up the rifle, aimed at the neck and squeezed the trigger in one instinctive motion. The seven-pointer crumpled, a mere twenty-two paces from where I stood.

As we mentioned before, the deer's best defense is its nose. Always respect it. When stalking, hunt into the wind, or quarter into a prevailing breeze, never have it on your back.

The hunter should also keep in mind that deer habitually feed into the wind. The generally accepted explanation for this is that the deer's hair lies back and the animal prefers to have the wind blowing over the hair naturally, rather than under the hair from the back. This is the deer's protection against the elements. It also gives the deer the advantage in that anything which crosses ahead will have its scent blown right to the deer's nose.

But take away its nose and the deer doesn't possess any super-plus advantage. Sure, its ears and eyes are sharp, with more latitude than those of the human's. Yet they aren't nearly as extraordinary as most people would believe. In the ordinary frequency of sound waves, in the range that humans detect, the deer can't hear a whole lot better than you or I. And the eyes are not so sensitive that the deer can stand off one hundred yards and see you crook your finger.

So when you have the wind in your favor, your chances of success are almost fifty-fifty, providing you plan your stalk properly. Of course, any deer is going to hear and see a hunter who blunders double time through the noisy woods, making no effort to conceal his sound or movement.

The foremost tendency among run-of-the-mill hunters is to walk fast. It is literally impossible to hunt too slowly. Sensible strategy is to hunt a small stretch of woods thoroughly and correctly, rather than to cover lots of terrain haphazardly.

When stalk hunting take one step and stand still for the count of two. After each step this means to stop briefly and look and listen. A deer has wonderful camouflage which causes it to blend almost perfectly with the background, but it often gives itself away by movement, either the raising of the head or a twitch of the tail. The hunter can also actually hear deer, the noises they make while moving around, if he can learn to listen for all the sounds of the woods, disregarding those which belong naturally in the environment, and detect those which play an integral part in his hunt.

I've been stalk hunting ever since I was old enough to tote a rifle. In the beginning I always wanted to keep moving, hunting hastily, trying to see as much country as I could. My father was continually harping on me to slow down. Finally, when I did discover for myself that I could kill many more deer and expend much less energy, only then did I slow down my pace and start hunting the way I should. I've never regretted it.

Actually, hunting too fast can be harmful. For the man who is used to sitting behind a desk throughout the year, getting out in the woods and trying to walk five or ten miles a day can have serious repercussions. Many men die out in the woods each year due to heart attacks. They simply weren't used to the extra exertion. So take it easy. You'll see more deer, come in at day's end feeling much better, and, who knows, maybe even save your life.

Footgear is important to the stalk hunter. Choose a boot with a soft sole, something that will absorb noise rather than reverberating it. Bird-hunting pacs are ideal for this kind of hunting. My veteran deer-hunting friend Guy Clymer goes this one further. He wears ordinary tennis shoes. He suffers with the cold, but he's the most uncanny and successful stalk hunter I've ever had the pleasure to watch in action. He'll bet you money he can walk right up on a deer, within twenty-five paces, and he'll win most every time.

When hunting hilly country, learn to slip quietly to the ridges and peek over to watch for deer on the opposite side. Learn to approach behind bushes or rocks to break your silhouette. The stalk hunter can't be too careful.

The best country, we repeat, for stalk hunting is that where there are few other hunters. The real secret of successful stalking is to be able to sneak up on unaware deer, perhaps one that is feeding. In country where

Stalking deer requires stealth and self-control. Take one step, stand still for the count of two and carefully observe the terrain. Always hunt facing into the wind so your scent is blown behind you.

heavy hunting pressure keeps the deer stirring about, they are going to be more spooky and more likely to detect the walking hunter.

Even in the most heavily hunted country, however, the wise deer hunter knows he can get a mile or so off public roads and have the country virtually to himself. The average American is a lazy and conservative hunter. He won't extend any extra effort toward getting his deer, and once out of sight of familiar landmarks, like the road, he becomes panicky because he fears getting lost. The hunter who is preoccupied with something else can't give stalk hunting the concentrated effort and undivided attention it demands.

When you head into the woods always carry a compass, particularly in strange terrain where landmarks are not familiar. Learn how to use it. Even the most observant hunters sometimes become lost, however. It is no disgrace to lose your way in this environment. The disgrace is to panic. Should you find yourself hopelessly turned around, fire the conventional three-shot lost signal and sit down and wait. Don't move. If someone knows where you are supposed to be, and this information should always be left with a relative or friend before you depart, then it won't be long before it is realized you are overdue and someone will come looking for you.

In this respect also remember to carry a supply of matches with you. They could come in handy, to build a fire for warming or for signaling.

In stalk hunting, many hunters miss their opportunities because of fatigue. Stalk hunting is walking. It is very tiring, particularly if you've been sitting

58

in an office all year and you're not used to the exercise. Fatigue can dull reflexes, and often just an instant of hesitation in that moment of truth when a deer is sighted, may make the difference between success and failure.

The wise hunter gets in shape for the deer season, especially if he has an office job and is out of shape. Since hunting is mostly walking, this exercise should be engaged in regularly for several weeks before going afield. Instead of jumping in the family auto for a trip to the nearby grocery, walk. Perhaps if your office isn't far away you can walk to and from work. Begin with a short distance and gradually increase it, adding a quarter mile about every second or third day. At the same time, step up the speed of hiking. In two or three weeks you should be able to clip off three or four miles without strain. Walking is one of the most healthful yet least strenuous of exercises.

In the week prior to the deer season, wear your regular field boots or shoes. This serves a twofold purpose. You get the footwear properly broken in and you become accustomed to the added weight. Walking a few flights of stairs daily will bring still other muscles into play. One of the best exercises I've found is to jog up and down the steps of the local football stadium.

If you're overweight, it also pays to take off a few extra pounds. You don't have to cut down on your food consumption to accomplish this. Just follow a high protein diet. Lay off starches and sweets. Eat plenty of meats and greaseless foods. The protein consumes fat. Being in shape for stalking not only intensifies the pleasures of the hunt, it also will make you more alert, quicker to spot game and take full advantage of your opportunities when they do beckon.

A popular method of stalk hunting, particularly in some Midwestern states, is by canoe or boat. Hunters put in on streams, on public land of course, and float with the current, scrutinizing both shorelines for deer. It is best if two hunters work as a team, one watching the left bank, the other the right. This is one of the most fascinating of all ways to hunt, and also one of the most productive since the hunter is covering lots of territory, yet making very little noise, and he's in wilderness country where there is apt to be much less hunting pressure.

The float hunter shouldn't expect to cover much territory in one single day. It is best to hunt a limited stretch slowly and thoroughly. A favorite system is to utilize two vehicles for the start and pickup. Get a map of the area. This information and other data on federal lands can be obtained from any of the regional offices, the addresses of which are listed below:

Write, Regional Office, U. S. Forest Service, at:
630 Sansome Street, San Francisco, California.
Forest Service Building, Ogden, Utah.
510 Second Street, N. W., Albuquerque, New Mexico.
710 N. Sixth Street, Milwaukee, Wisconsin.
50 Seventh Street, Atlanta, Georgia.
6816 Market Street, Upper Darby, Pennsylvania.
Federal Building, Missoula, Montana.
Federal Center Building 85, Denver 7, Colorado.

Once you have an accurate map, you can lay out a hunt, finding the best spot to put in and the best spot to take out.

If it is other than federal land, go to the respective agency which controls hunting and attempt to obtain maps. For state land, inquire of the state conservation department. Private land, deal directly with the landowner. If it is some timber company which has opened its spread to deer hunting, obtain a map from the headquarters of that company. Many such companies welcome hunters and some of these lands offer the best hunting to be found anywhere, thanks to wise habitat management. A couple of pertinent examples are the Sinnissippi Forest Tree Farm at Oregon, Illinois, and the International Paper Company in the Adirondacks of New York, near Speculator.

Now you're ready to go. Take both vehicles, each hunter driving one, to the spot where you expect to terminate your hunt. Park one there and drive the other to the starting point. This way transportation will be available when you arrive. Some hunters plan on several days afloat, pausing on the way downstream to camp along the stream shore, maybe mixing in a little fishing with the hunting. But one note of caution. Before camping, check on local regulations. In some national forests, camping is restricted to supervised campgrounds, and in some, you must obtain a permit to build a campfire. Always be sure you're within the law before building a camp anywhere.

At times stalk hunting can be very productive; other times, stand hunting is the only logical way to hunt. Often, then, the ideal system is a blend of the two. Some hunters sit on a stand until they feel they must move, then stalk hunt until their muscles unwind and their blood is circulating freely again, then they look for another stand to wait a spell.

Bill Klapp likes to tell about the time when such a plan paid off handsomely. Bill is owner of the Original Sight-Exchange Company in Paoli, Pennsylvania, and a deer hunter of skill. Here's how he describes this particular hunt:

"Ralph Buffett, a gunsmith, and I were hunting in the Seven Mountains Range of the Allegheny Mountains in Center County, Pennsylvania, in Shingletown Gap. It was opening day of the season and we started hunting, Ralph and I, up the side of a mountain. There was snow on the ground which made for quiet traveling. It also was about two degrees below zero, uncomfortably cold to sit on a stand for any length of time; so I figured we'd stalk hunt a while, then sit down and watch until we got cold before getting up and moving again.

"I went ahead about one hundred yards beyond Ralph, figuring that other hunters I knew camped up on top of the mountain might spook some deer down our way, and if one should come down and see me before I could get a shot, it might swerve and sneak across behind me, affording Ralph a shot.

"Here the mountains go almost straight up, to about 2,300 feet elevation, and it was tough walking. I also had to move very slowly to watch in the heavy cover. Hardwoods like hickory, beechnut, spruce and pine grow profusely on the mountainsides, and there is a lot of rhododendron and laurel for ground covering. It is very difficult to see a deer in this underbrush.

"We'd gone up the mountain trail for maybe two or three miles when I heard a shot behind me. I turned around and hurried back and found Ralph bending over a nice six-point buck lying in the laurel at the edge of the trail. Our strategy had worked out perfectly and Ralph had dropped the buck with a single shot from his .32 Remington.

"We gutted the deer and took it back to the car. Then we headed up the same trail again. After walking this time for about five miles, I decided to sit down, catch my breath and do a little stand hunting. In a few minutes I heard a twig snap and shortly two deer, a small one and a large one, came into view, walking up the trail. I raised my .35 Remington, peered through the Lyman Alaskan scope and noticed the big one had a large set of horns.

"One shot in the heart region did it. And I tell you, when we drove out with a buck on each fender of the car, we got a lot of envious glances from other hunters."

This is one instance when a contributing factor, the weather, dictated a combination of stand and stalk hunting. There are other such factors. Like the habits of deer, for instance. During a typical hunting day, the deer will be up and about early in the morning and late in the day, feeding and watering. The tendency then is for them to bed down in the mid-day hours. To allow for this behavior, the strategy would be to stand hunt in the early morning and late afternoon, when deer are up and moving about, and stalk hunting during those hours when the critters are resting in the underbrush, hoping to roust one from its bed for a shot.

Favorite bedding spots for deer are along timbered and brush-covered ridges and in the swamps. The hunter who jumps a deer from its bed can expect, usually, to get only a fleeting, running shot at the animal. This kind of hunting demands a hunter who can size up a situation in a split-second and be able to adapt himself accordingly.

Most hunters overestimate the speed of a deer. They tend to lead running animals too much. The system I prefer is to swing the gun in the direction the deer is moving, pulling up until the sight centers on the neck before firing. This way the movement of the gun will be in synchronization with the running deer, and a bullet fired at the neck, discounting the time lapse it takes a hunter's reflexes to react, will usually hit the animal somewhere in the shoulder region.

Tracking is another method of hunting deer. In a way, it is an offshoot of stalking. It is, basically, nothing more than following tracks, hoping to get a shot at whatever is making those tracks.

This system is, at its best, only a long-shot affair. I once read a newspaper account of a hunter in the Cedar Stream area of New Hampshire who spent almost two full days on a deer spoor. He got on the trail early one morning, kept after it all day, marked the spot near nightfall where he quit the track, returned the following morning and dogged the deer for almost another full day before bagging a big buck just at sundown.

Me, I don't have that kind of perseverance. Yet that's what it takes. The hunter must stick with it if he is to track down a deer. It is no easy feat.

Roused by a stalking hunter from its mid-day nap, a whitetail buck presents only a fleeting target as it bounds into the under-brush. Stalking is most productive during the day when the deer are bedded down. *Courtesy Nebraska Game Commission.*

The trouble is, the hunter often doesn't know how old a track may be. Perhaps he will take out on a trail that was made the previous day. Naturally, his chances of getting a shot at that particular animal are almost nil.

There is one time, however, when tracking definitely pays off. Suppose you were driving down a country lane when a buck jumped across the road in front of you. This is a hot track. Get right on it and mind your ABC's of tracking and the odds are in your favor that you'll get a shot.

Another good time for track searching is just after a fresh snowfall. Should a new layer of the white stuff be added to the ground overnight, you'll know that any tracks you come across are fresh.

And, with apologies for sounding too pessimistic, there is still another deterent to the tracker. Often he doesn't know if he is trailing a buck or a doe. In areas where either is legal, this isn't important. But it is to the hunter out exclusively for a buck.

The male and female deer do make different tracks, but it requires an experienced eye sometimes to ascertain the difference. A big track doesn't necessarily mean it was left by a buck, yet usually it has been. But the main characteristics to watch for are toeing-out of the front feet, one mark of the buck, and a gait that shows the front feet wider apart. If there are two sets of tracks, doe and buck, you can readily tell the difference. A buck tends to drag his forefeet in light snow, while a doe has this tendency only in deeper snow. The doe almost invariably puts the print of her back feet directly over those of the forefeet, while bucks often do not, and a buck will show some spreading between the two halves of the forefeet when walking naturally, while does do this only when running.

Tracking is a fascinating way to hunt deer and is possible in any area where snow falls during the season, from Oregon and Washington across the Great Lakes states into the East. But remember that deer also are aware they are leaving a telltale traveling card with their tracks and they are much more wary and alert when there is snow on the ground. They are continually watching their backtrack, and the hunter must be doubly cautious.

Should the tracks lead into a thicket, this might be where the deer has elected to bed down. It often pays to skirt the thicket, searching for outcoming tracks. If there are none, the deer probably is still in there and you can work to spook him out where you stand the best chance of getting an open shot. Another thing to keep in mind is the wind. Perhaps while you are trying to circle the thicket, you'll cross the prevailing breeze, sweeping your scent right into the thicket. Should this happen, probably all you'll hear is a crashing noise meaning the buck has fled for freedom.

Tracking paid off with the biggest whitetail killed in 1963 and the fourth largest typical head ever recorded. Earl T. McMaster of Columbia Falls, Montana, got this one in the foothills along the fringe of the continental divide near Columbia Mountain in Montana. He first saw the huge buck standing alongside the road. Later, he returned, located the deer's tracks, and stealthily followed the telltale spoor through fresh snow. Sometime afterwards he came upon the deer in a clump of brush and killed it. The antlers scored 191 5/8 points in Boone and Crockett Club competition.

Since a deer being tracked, and aware that a human is on its trail, has a tendency to keep moving and out of sight, often hunters sort of combine tracking and stand hunting to ambush the wary animal. This is a popular method throughout the Midwest. A hunter or two will remain on the deer's trail while other hunters circle ahead and take stands, hoping to intercept the deer as the trackers push it along.

There are many variations of this. One produced the largest buck ever killed in Ohio. Arlee McCullough of Newark, Ohio, got it, a trophy that measured 186 2/8 points. He'd tracked the buck and some does for a few hours one afternoon. Just at dusk, the deer entered a large stand of brush. McCullough figured this was where the animals would bed for the night. Early the following morning he picked a strategic spot where he could watch the brush and sat down and waited. Soon something or someone spooked the deer. They came running from the brush. McCullough got on the big buck with his Marlin shotgun loaded with rifled slugs and hit it twice running.

As with conventional stalking, the tracker must accept the fact that most of his chances will be at running deer, unless he's particularly adept at setting up the animal for a standing shot. Usually the deer sights the hunter, rather than vice versa. The hunter will see the game, all right, but by the time he does, the deer will be on the retreat. Running deer aren't too difficult to hit, but the hunter must have confidence in his ability and must know how to handle his firearm properly under such conditions.

During the summer months some friends and I like to play self-styled games of shooting which condition our reflexes for the upcoming autumn deer seasons. To simulate a running deer, we insert a piece of cardboard in the hole of an old automobile tire. One man stands on an incline, perhaps the side of a hill, and starts the tire rolling down. He then steps behind some sort of protection like a large boulder or tree, for obvious reasons. The tire comes bounc-

To develop accuracy in leading running deer, practice with an automobile tire rigged with a target and rolled down a gentle slope. Most hunters tend to lead a deer too much. Swing with the animal and aim at the neck region for a hit in the shoulder area.

ing erratically, building up momentum as it speeds on its downward course. The hunter stands off to one side and fires at the cardboard insert in the moving object.

In some places, commercial ranges are being constructed to allow hunters, who pay fees, to shoot at realistic deer targets as they move in an erratic circular pattern on a track.

Another game we play is devised by painting silhouettes on large squares of cardboard (those cartons that mattresses come packed in are ideal). Normally, we try to paint up about twelve such silhouettes. On four cardboard squares are sketched the outlines of humans; on the rest are painted deer.

One person, in advance, goes along a game trail and hides the cardboard squares in upright positions, in inconspicuous places but still visible from the trail. Then the other person, armed, catfoots along the trail, searching for the silhouettes, which can be painted in actual colors to further simulate true hunting conditions. When he spots one of the silhouettes, he first must determine whether or not it is legal game, a deer not a human, and then, if it is a deer, he must get off a shot as quickly as possible (our time limit is ten seconds). The person who scores the most hits is the winner. Should there be a tie, then the person who puts the greatest number of shots in vital areas is declared the champ.

But shooting is just one facet of this game. It is equally important that the hunter be taught to make sure of his target before pulling the trigger. Just because there is no visible bright clothing is no reason for shooting. The hunter should never, never fire at an object just because he believes it to be a deer.

To protect himself, the hunter also should take precautions to make himself readily visible to other hunters. This means wearing bright clothing. The time-honored brilliant reds and yellows are still good. But even better are fluorescent "blaze-orange" and fluorescent "neon-red." This was discovered in a series of exhaustive tests at Fort Devons, Massachusetts, to determine which colors afford hunters the best protection. The advantage of both these fluorescent colors is that they can be distinguished by color-blind people, who comprise something like eight per cent of the total population.

These games make for fascinating sport during the idle months, and in the long run they assure more shooting success in the field and improve your ability to distinguish game from other landmarks.

9   Driving and Calling

ORGANIZATION OFTEN pays off in deer hunting as well as it does in a business venture. Through teamwork, hunters frequently can get shots at deer when they'd only draw blanks if attempting to go it alone.

Bill Klapp is a staunch believer in "driving" deer. This veteran Pennsylvania hunter says that a drive properly executed can be one of the most effective of all ways to put venison in the deepfreeze.

Let's listen to him tell about an instance when it paid off for him and his companions:

"We were hunting near Greentown, Pike County, Pennsylvania, in the foothills. This was during the antlerless deer season in that area, and there were six of us in the party.

"The foothill country of Pike County is mostly rolling forest land interspersed with farms and a considerable amount of rhododendron swamps and thickets. The spot we picked to hunt was a sprawling rhododendron thicket maybe 300 yards wide and a half-mile long. Evidence of deer travel was in the thicket in the form of tunnel-like passages where deer would crouch and almost crawl along the well-worn trails.

"Doyle Johnson and Bill Rhinehart said they would do the driving while the rest of us stationed ourselves along the sides and end of the thicket to intercept any deer which might be flushed out. Johnson and Rhinehart circled to the opposite end of the thicket and began working their way through the tunnel-like passages.

"I was on one side of the thicket holding my .35 Remington rifle equipped with a Lyman Alaskan $2\frac{1}{2}$X scope. In a little while, I heard a commotion in the thicket and moments later a bear with two cubs came lumbering out. The bear season was closed and I allowed them to pass. Just a few short minutes later, four deer, two bucks and two does, came bounding out. They ran across a small clearing where Tim McAvoy was hiding, and I expected any second to hear a shot.

"Nothing. I kept wondering what possibly could have happened. Finally,

I figured he'd failed to see the deer and I lined up on the lead doe and knocked her over. Almost simultaneously, a roar came from Tim's direction and the tail-end buck cartwheeled. Then I heard another shot from the other side of the thicket.

"I walked down and looked where my deer had fallen. Then I went back to where Tim was standing over his kill. I asked him what happened. He said he hesitated because he couldn't get the deer in his scope, but he finally did just as I fired. One of the hunters on the other side of the clearing also scored. That particular drive paid off with three deer in a little more than an hour's time."

In a place like Pennsylvania, the hunter has his choice of using whatever method he prefers to get his deer. But there are some isolated instances when a well-planned drive is almost demanded if the hunters are to succeed. A good example is the Louisiana swamp country. Here men can't move about in pursuit of deer, it being practically impossible because of the quagmirelike terrain. Specially trained dogs are used to push the deer toward standers stationed in strategic positions to intercept any bucks rousted from the swampy marshes by the hounds, which can be of almost any breed. Such hound strains as Walkers, blueticks and black and tans are among the favorites. In Arkansas, many deer hunters employ beagle hounds. They say these short-legged dogs are ideal for this kind of hunting since they keep the deer stirring, yet because they are slow, they don't excite the animals as much and don't drive them out of the country. One special kind of dog used in Louisiana is the Catahoula hound, named after Catahoula Parish where it is used extensively by deer hunters. This hound was developed by the crossbreeding and interbreeding of many hound strains to get a dog especially adapted to swamp country.

Driving with dogs is frowned upon in most deer-hunting areas, but in some circumstances the canine assistance not only is helpful, it is necessary. And deer hunting in the wild and forbidding swamp country, is about as exciting a sport as a person could find anywhere.

Drive hunting can be of various forms. As few as two people can drive deer successfully. Or maybe as many as twenty or thirty will be employed.

Bill Klapp tells about another time when he and H. Wilson Orr were hunting in Huntingdon County, Pennsylvania. They were hunting around a large apple orchard where the farmer said many deer had been coming to eat the fruit and feed on his young trees. Along one side of the orchard were the foothills of the Allegheny Mountains. While hunting around the orchard, Klapp happened to glance up on one of the hills and noticed a large buck crossing through a clearing and disappearing into a thicket.

The hunters assumed the deer had entered the thicket to bed down. Hastily, working out a strategy, the hunters decided that Orr would hide in some bushes down from the thicket while Klapp would circle to the opposite side and attempt to flush the buck out for a shot.

After reaching a point on the other side of the knoll, just down from the thicket, Klapp commenced to walk a zigzag course up the knoll, making as much noise as possible. Sure enough, in a few minutes Klapp heard a shot and when he reached the place where Orr had been hiding, his companion was busy field-dressing the big buck. The strategy had worked out just as planned. Orr said the deer simply walked down the knoll, stopped and looked back. A single shot from a .30/06 did the job.

One of the first deer I ever killed blundered unsuspectingly right into an ambush, a hastily conceived scheme where I actually had the buck driven to me. It was no great shakes of a drive, mind you, but nothing more elaborate nor more carefully planned could have worked out any better.

O. D. Tinsley, my father, and I jumped a group of deer, three does and a forkhorn buck, from a small brushy header. We caught just a flash of them topping the ridge and disappearing on the yonder side. Dad, being familiar with the country, knew the deer were crossing over into a deep-slashed canyon choked with cedar trees. If we gave immediate chase there would be little hope for a shot at the wily brush-wise animals.

But Dad, who has killed more deer in a lifetime of hunting thán he'd care to admit, knows the behavior of whitetails, how they react under specific circumstances. This knowledge proved to be the downfall of the buck.

Dad instructed me to work down the header and circle until I came to the mouth of the canyon, find a vantage point and watch the canyon mouth. Chances are the deer would stay in the cover, he explained, not moving any farther. At least that's what he was gambling on.

After twenty minutes lapse, enough time for me to get into position, Dad would climb over the ridge and down into the canyon. He'd hunt slowly along the floor toward the mouth. The deer, he figured, would probably slip down the canyon, staying within the protection of the cover and moving quietly to conceal their retreat. If things worked out according to plan, the buck should pass just below where I waited impatiently in ambush.

Dad turned out to be a prophet. About halfway down the canyon, he must have spooked the deer, for I saw the three panicked does angling up the opposite side and topping out on the ridge. But there was no sign of the buck.

Minutes later, I heard a clicking of stones in the dry-washed innards of the canyon. Shortly, the phanthom-like buck eased into view, stepping lightly, head tucked down, sneaking from the canyon. It was almost too easy. I guess that's why I missed with my first try, overshot. But fortunately the deer didn't scare.

Instead, he threw up his head alertly, searching for whatever caused the commotion. The second shot from my .30/30 staggered him. He ran a couple of dozen yards before piling up limply against a small oak tree.

These are two examples of the crudest form of driving, employing only two drivers, yet the method that is most widely used by deer hunters. A successful drive can be organized by as many hunters as may be handy. In the pine barrens of New Jersey, a far-reaching drive might include forty or fifty hunters.

But no matter where it is staged or how many participants are involved, the drive has one basic purpose: to move deer in a designated pattern in order to set them up for standers situated at predetermined vantage points.

One variation of this is a drive where no standers are involved, being composed simply of a string of hunters fanned out across the countryside. Perhaps each one will follow parallel logging roads or laid-out compass courses, traveling at about the same slow speed so the line will sweep across the deer habitat at an even pace.

The whitetail deer is an animal of fairly restricted range. It is reluctant to leave its home territory. Thus, when being driven ahead of the hunter line, it will frequently try to circle around and backtrack, sneaking behind the human to enter its bailiwick. This is just what the line of hunters hopes to accomplish. The deer skirting away from one hunter might cross paths with another hunter in the drive, and a mistake like this could be fatal. But in a drive such as this, safety precautions should be stressed. One hunter should never fire in the direction of another driver. All shots should be out front or in the rear, never to either side.

In broken country of draws and headers, two or three persons can launch a successful drive. Deer always tend to move with the wash, either exiting from its mouth or its beginning. Therefore, should the driver enter the draw from

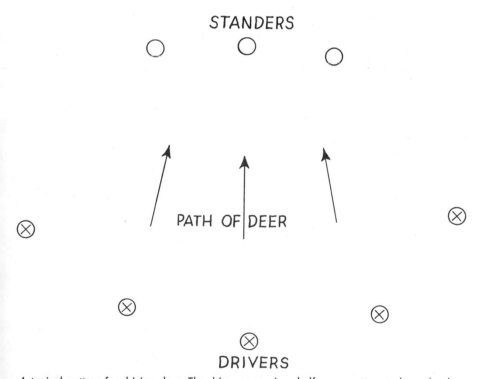

A typical pattern for driving deer. The drivers move in a half-moon pattern to keep the deer from slipping around their flanks. The standers should be stationed along runs the deer are likely to take as they move ahead of the drivers.

above, the beginning, the stander should be set up in a concealed position where the draw opens its mouth.

At least one person in the party must be intimately acquainted with the terrain. They should know the major deer runs, the likely routes deer will follow when fleeing the drivers. The very success of the drive depends on having the standers at the right places at the right time. A drive pattern is sort of triangular shaped, with the standers set up at the apex of the triangle and the drivers fanned out along its base. Rather than a straight line, the drivers should move in a half-moon sweep, the outside drivers being slightly ahead of the others to discourage deer from breaking through either side of the drive line.

Stands must be situated so that each one is out of the line of fire of the others. Shotguns are popular in this type of hunting since most shots tend to be at running deer at close range, and the short-range weapons offer more safety precautions.

The drivers also should be alert for deer, not depending on them all to travel as predicted. Sometimes, they'll try to double back. Doyle Johnson recalls a time when he was slipping through a thicket in Pike County, Pennsylvania, attempting to drive the deer out for others in his party to get shots, when suddenly three deer came running down the thicket-lined trail and like to have trampled him. The first deer sighted the hunter and tried to stop, planting both forefeet, but the other two crashed into the first, and the tangle of deer slammed into the thicket, scrambling frantically to escape. Doyle was too dumbfounded even to get his gun up for a shot.

There are basically two ways to conduct a drive. One is to have the drivers steal along quietly, hoping to get a shot at deer themselves, and the other is to have them create a loud ruckus to move the deer on and prevent them from doubling back through the driving line.

The idea is not to be in too much of a hurry. Deer should not be driven out on the run; rather, they should be prompted just to slip away, moving along slowly so they are apt to be spotted by standers in time for a shot and so there will be better chances of a kill.

The secret of a successful drive is organization. It is important that one or two persons be put in charge of the hunt, to organize and plan it, placing the standers and drivers in the most strategic positions. A disorderly drive not only cuts down on the deer kill, it also is dangerous.

Calling deer with commercial calls, blown by mouth, is relatively new to the sport and there is still some doubt as to their consistent effectiveness, especially with whitetail deer. Bill Klapp says he has used such calls with a good deal of success in Pennsylvania, but most reports from hunters I've received detailed only spotty results. But one form of calling—rattlin'—is almost as old as deer hunting itself.

Rattlin' a buck in close, within gunshot range, can be accomplished anywhere the rut or mating season comes simultaneously with the legal hunting season. It is particularly effective in that area called the brush country of

Rattling a pair of antlers during the rutting season will often bring a buck within gunshot range. The antlers are banged and twisted together, even rapped against trees and brush, to simulate the battling of bucks.

South Texas, a he-man terrain of bushes with exotic Mexican names, plants that all have one thing in common—thorns.

When the bucks are running does, which usually occurs in December in southern Texas, rattlin' is a deadly method for bringing the belligerent males to you, the hunter. One of the most successful "rattlers" I know is Dr. Raleigh R. Ross, a surgeon friend of mine.

He prefers a set of matched mule deer antlers rather than whitetail deer antlers, because the muley racks tend to be straight, while the whitetail's have a curve inward, making it more difficult to slam them together to simulate two bucks fighting.

The antlers are sawed off the deer's head right at the base and allowed to season or dry out. A set about a year old is right. When they get too dried out, they have an artificial ring. They are tied together with a piece of cord and slung over the shoulder, for easy portage.

Contrary to popular belief, antlers are not rattled together with the tine points facing each other, as they appear on the deer's head. Rather, the points go in the same direction, with the curve of one antler banged against the curve of the other.

The antlers are slammed together violently, twisted back and forth, banged together again hard. Occasionally, the hunter will even use them to pound on nearby brush and against the ground. Sound effects are important. When two bucks square off they really set up a hair-raising commotion.

Dr. Ross likes to tell about a big buck he rattled up in South Texas a few seasons back. It was a cold December morning with hoar frost on the ground and spiny bushes and a light ice-edged wind blowing.

"I took this fellow out and told him I'd try to rattle him in a buck. Right after I started pounding the antlers together I saw a deer off in the brush, just his bobbing antlers sticking up where I could see them. He was a big one, all right, but I couldn't get him to come on in.

"This friend of mine never did see the buck until suddenly the critter decided he'd had enough. He just couldn't stand it any longer. With a wild look in his eyes, he came charging out of the brush, kicking up dust like a mad bull. Man, you should have seen that fellow's face when this large buck ran unexpectedly right up within twenty paces of where he was sitting in the fork of a tree. He like to have forgot to shoot he was so excited and dumb-founded."

Another accomplished caller, one Leroy Liberda of Austin, Texas, says when a hunter uses light antlers and bangs them together steadily, he is most likely to bring in the smaller bucks. For mean, belligerent, big bucks, use heavy antlers and wham them together slowly, but with great force.

The problem with rattling is getting a buck to hear the noise. The sound won't carry much more than a quarter of a mile, which means you must be within close proximity of a deer to rattle it up. Bob Ramsey, a Real County, Texas, rancher, is acknowledged as one of the best at beguiling trophy bucks with slammed-together antlers. He says a clear, cold, still morning, one where sound will carry, is best.

Deer react to rattling in different ways. An eager one might plough right on in, blood in his eye. A warier one might sneak around, looking and listening, reluctant to come closer. Often, in this case, Ramsey beats on the ground and slams brush with the antlers, to give the impression of a heated fight. The idea is to work on the buck's emotions until he can't stand it any longer.

Rattling will work anywhere the rut corresponds with the season and there is a high ratio of bucks to does. If the ratio is one-sided, many more does than bucks, the males don't have to fight over the affections of the females. In southern Texas, where many trophy heads have been taken, it is particularly productive because the dense, head-high brush makes it difficult to hunt in any other way. A buck can remain effectively hidden in the thorny brush unless he is inveigled into exposing himself.

Luring deer in with mouth-blown calls, despite some success, still is much in the experimental stage, particularly with whitetails. Murry and Winston Burnham, the brothers of game-calling fame who have done much research into the behavior of wild animals and which sounds cause them to react, tell me that whitetails sometimes will come to a call, though the results are unpredictable.

The tone of a deer call is similar in sound to that made by the dying-rabbit predator call, but the pitch of the deer call is much lower. This pitch is important. The deer caller has to create just the right sound to entice a deer to come a-running.

The call the Burnhams have developed to bring in the bucks is a weird-sounding thing, violent and loud with an anguished squeal. This is a star-tlingly different sound from the one the brothers first started with, an imitation of a soft-bleating fawn. The distressful bleating, they discovered, will often bring a wild-eyed doe in fast, but it never enjoyed much success on bucks.

The loud, panicky sound is much more effective, which is odd since the deer is one of the least loquacious of all wild animals. The Burnhams' theory is that the call arouses the curiosity of a buck.

Numerous times I've had deer answer the squalling of a rabbit-in-distress predator call while hunting in my central Texas bailiwick and in Mexico. It isn't unusual to have a pugnacious doe come bolting out of the brush, run up close and start pawing the ground and snorting. Probably she associates the gosh-awful noise with some sort of danger to her young.

One thing the Burnhams found was that the calling should be abruptly terminated when a buck approaches within view. The calling when the animal has approached fairly close often drives him off, rather than luring him. The distress call normally works best in the fall on the bucks, but at times the males will come to a soft, bleating sound, like a doe often calls during the rut.

The Burnhams said one Pennsylvania game-calling enthusiast, James S. Seibel of Pittsburgh, wrote them that he has called and kept records on more than 900 deer in his home state, which proves that the system can be effective if the caller knows what he is doing.

The caller should use all the caution of the stand hunter, staying concealed and completely still, with the wind blowing in his face. A day with little or no wind is best for calling, the Burnhams explain, because a stiff breeze muffles the call, and also it throws the human scent away where deer can detect it. And one note of caution. Be sure and check the game laws in your respective state to see if deer calls are allowed. In some states they are illegal.

No matter which method you may choose to seek your deer—stand hunting, stalking, tracking, driving or calling—always take the positive approach and have confidence in your own ability. If you follow the rules outlined here, there is no reason why you shouldn't get your deer this season. Every year beginners with no prior experience go afield and score, some of them with quite spectacular results.

Orrie L. Schaeffer of Corning, Missouri, is a living example of this. In 1962, on his very first deer hunt in Holt County, Schaeffer downed a ten-point buck which weighed nearly 300 pounds. Just getting a deer on his first hunt was significant enough, but Schaeffer had the added distinction of downing the largest whitetail buck (by Boone and Crockett Club measurements) ever to be killed in the state of Missouri.

10 Hunting the Storm Fronts

DAILY HABITS of whitetail deer fall into a fairly predictable pattern. On a typical seasonal day the deer will feed through much of the night on until sunup, or shortly thereafter, before heading for protective cover to bed down. Sometime in the afternoon, the animals will steal from the cover again to feed and water, on into the night. There will be a variation in the ratio of how long the deer are up to how long they remain bedded down, depending on many factors like weather and phases of the moon, but basically this is the pattern the whitetail will follow, up early and late, down during the mid-day hours.

But there are some days when deer are moving about almost continuously. They either don't bed down at all or for a very short time. It may be a mild, sunny day, not unlike the previous day when the deer followed their regular routine, yet there will be evidence of movement everywhere. It is a phenomenon which every observant hunter takes into consideration when mapping his strategy.

I remember one of those rare days at the opening of the deer season a few years back. It was a beautiful, sunny fall day, clear and still. My stand was in the high fork of a gnarled oak tree overlooking a well-traveled deer run. I can't recall ever seeing more deer than I did that morning. In fact, by noon I'd glimpsed four legal bucks; each time something crossed me up and prevented me from getting an early, auspicious start to the season. Three times I had no control over the matter, the deer being in situations which handicapped me, such as the time one walked through a sliver of opening allowing just a quick glimpse for identification, but not enough time for a reasonable shot. But the other muffed opportunity was of my own doing. I had a deer standing about seventy-five yards away and blew the golden chance by overshooting.

For every buck I sighted, however, I must have counted at least four or five does, fawns and yearlings. Hardly was there a time when I didn't have at least one deer within my vision. Often there were two or three feeding near my makeshift tree stand.

Soon after noon, around one o'clock, I was preoccupied with watching a pair of female deer grazing off to my right, when a noise of hoofs on rocks behind me quickly diverted my attention. I looked around just in time to see a nice buck scrambling through a dry wash, kicking rocks as he jumped in and out. He was walking directly away from me as I put the sight on his back, just this side of the shoulder, and touched 'er off. The bullet struck fair just where I was aiming, angled down through the chest cavity and exited in front of the shoulders. That buck was dead before he hit the ground.

That shot abruptly terminated my hunting for the day, but all the other hunters I talked with later remarked about the unusual deer movement, right on through the warm mid-day hours, when normally the animals would be lost in the cover.

The next morning I knew the answer. The kind of storm that we Texans have come to call a "blue norther" came snowballing in from the north, gaining momentum as it went, a severe storm for so early in the year. An icy wind sent the temperature plummeting below the freezing mark, and for three days the storm raged.

It explained the deer movement. A creature of the wild seems to have a built-in "sixth sense" when it comes to forecasting weather. The deer, with its limited protection against the elements, owes its very existence to its ability to foretell what weather the days ahead will bring. The deer on this particular season opener were up and about throughout the day, feeding, to get ready for the lean storm days ahead when they would be relatively confined.

That season opener was one of the best in history with a heavy kill of deer. Yet the following day the number of animals being brought into the small deer-hunting towns dropped drastically. The deer had migrated back into the dense cover, seeking protection from the storm, and there was only limited movement.

After the weather front moved on southward, skies cleared and temperatures began climbing again, and the deer ventured back out to browse and water. The day after the severe storm was a time of movement again. The weather was fifteen to twenty degrees colder than it was opening day, yet still not severe enough to keep the deer in the cover. Right on through the noon hour, the animals were still milling about, feeding.

Again, the deer were following a predictable pattern based on the weather outlook.

Just prior to a severe storm, and again right after, there will be concentrated deer movement. Before the bad weather, the deer are storing up food, filling their bellies, in anticipation of the lean days ahead, days when they will be relatively confined. After the storm, the deer will come out to stuff their empty stomachs. This behavior is particularly noticeable before severe fronts which bring abrupt changes in weather. Perhaps the sudden change will be in the form of cold severe weather or maybe it will be torrential rains. If it is the kind of weather which will interfere with the deer's daily habits, then it will aid the hunter, helping him to plan his strategy according to the anticipated reactions of the deer to the weather change.

A deer is a whole lot like humans in this respect. Weather dictates what its routine will be, not vice versa. Everything it does is directly influenced by weather because in the wilds an abrupt change in the elements often is fatal to the less hardy creatures.

Suppose a severe storm blows in, bringing with it snow and hard-freezing temperatures. In this kind of inclement weather, a deer isn't going to feed into the night, although otherwise it is a nocturnal creature, because it would rather bed down to find some protection against the night cold, and feed when the sun is up.

The duration of the storm also is a determining factor on deer movement. With storms of short duration, two or three days, the deer will remain restricted to a fairly limited area, not moving around much; but should the storm last for many days, the deer will venture out to feed and water at times, but the movement won't be nearly as pronounced as it is during more typical weather.

Sometimes there is an overlap which brings phenomenal hunting. Just after a storm hits, for example, the deer might be at the peak of their feeding spree, heading for cover only as the storm gains in intensity.

There are many hunters who swear by the barometer. Their philosophy is this: high barometer, good hunting; low barometer, poor hunting.

A barometer, of course, is only a device for predicting weather. Generally, a high barometer will mean fair weather, a low barometer will indicate bad weather. It is this elementary.

Immediately after a storm, when the barometer is rising steadily, there is often a time for exceptional hunting. I remember one particular New Mexico rain storm, a steady wintery drizzle which lasted for two miserable days. On the third day the black clouds scattered and the skies opened up as blue as the eyes of a newborn baby, and the sun sparkled like diamonds on the rain-splattered trees.

Right after a rainstorm is one of my pet times for still hunting. The ground is soggy and quiet, making for silent traveling. And the deer are moving about freely, exposing themselves in a more vulnerable position.

On this morning in the woods, the first thing I noticed was the unmistakable evidence of deer movement. Fresh tracks were everywhere. In the moist earth, after the storm, the telltale tracks showed up vividly, and since the rain had washed all past evidence away, I knew the tracks had been made at least the night before, no sooner.

Throughout the day I sighted untold numbers of deer. Many of the feeding animals, I walked right up on. This was in the pine forests of Lincoln National Forest, near Cloudcroft, an area where I'd hunted only a week earlier and found very little evidence of deer.

The weather had made the difference. It had prompted the deer to move about more, to track up the area.

Weather also influences the hunter's strategy. As a general rule, stand hunting will be more productive immediately prior to and immediately after the storm, since these will be times of active deer movement. During the storm, the hunter must still hunt back among the dense cover, hoping to jump deer from their beds.

The wise hunter keeps close check on weather reports. He knows when the fronts are moving in, the nature of them, and how to incorporate the anticipated weather changes into his hunting strategy.

In populous areas where deer-hunting pressure is greatest, the weather is a definite asset. A deer preparing for unsettled weather, or regrouping after a storm, is going to be less cautious and more vulnerable to the hunter. The more severe the incoming storm, the more concentrated and heavy will be the deer movement, and the easier and more predictable is the hunter's job.

11 Advanced Deer Hunting

WHEN DEL AUSTIN bagged his world-record whitetail (archery non-typical) in the Platte River bottoms of Nebraska, south of Shelton, he afterwards attributed much of his good fortune to luck. In 1962, Austin and a companion, Charlie Marlowe, decided to go after the big buck one afternoon. Austin stationed himself alongside a good deer run, in a tree blind, on the Dan Thomas farm. Some thirty minutes later, he heard a crashing noise in the brush and shortly the big buck stepped into the open. When he was a scant twenty yards away, Austin pulled back on his bow and let an arrow fly. It was a solid hit behind the front leg and—presto!—Austin had himself first place in the Pope and Young Club (tabulators of archery records) book.

True, Lady Luck does play an important role in deer hunting, particularly when a man collects a record trophy head. It is the old axiom of being at the right place at the right time. But it goes deeper than that. Occasionally, a novice will bag a big buck, but usually such a specimen will fall before the seasoned veteran hunters, those who have the know-how and skill to outwit a super-sly whitetail.

Take Austin and his record kill, for instance. The hunter knew enough to station himself along a known deer run, where he had the best chance of spotting deer. He knew enough to conceal himself thoroughly and avoid detection. But more important, he was aware that the big buck roamed the area. Austin had been told by Al Dawson that he had seen the giant buck for the five previous seasons in the Platte River country, in the vicinity where Austin elected to hunt.

This incident points up something about the behavior of whitetail deer which few hunters realize. The whitetail is an animal of a limited area. When it homesteads on a certain place, usually the area where it was born and raised, it remains mostly within that area, never ranging far away. This is why one tract can have a serious overpopulation of deer with a drastic die-off because of a food deficiency, while maybe a mile away there might be a comparable area with only a nominal population.

Dr. William B. Davis, a professor of wildlife management at Texas A&M University, says that "normally when food conditions are adequate, deer tend to stay in one locality for long periods."

Just how limited this locality usually is was revealed in a study of trapping and retrapping deer by the Texas Game and Fish Commission. One particular example was a buck that was killed within sight of the trapping site where it was caught, banded and released five years earlier.

In another phase of this program, 102 deer were captured, tagged and released. Of this number, forty-three were caught again, and all but three were taken in the same traps. Another time, forty-nine deer were retrapped from an original sixty-six tagged, and not one was taken more than a quarter of a mile away, many in the same traps.

Nineteen deer were tagged in another phase and in twelve retraps, the average distance between point of release and recapture was a mere sixty-three yards. In three specific examples, deer were recaught in the same traps with time lapses of 15½, 15 and 16½ months respectively.

A somewhat different project in Florida reaffirmed these findings. At Eglin Air Force Base, several deer were equipped with radio transmittors. The deer had been captured by the use of a dart gun which delivers a temporary anesthetic to the animal. Then the deer were fitted with a harness which carries a compact but strong radio transmittor. Through the use of telemetry, the deer's daily progress was mapped. Preliminary findings revealed that the daily wandering of a deer was less than a mile.

What this means to the hunter is that if he can pinpoint the spot where a shootable deer is ranging, he can fairly well assume the deer will remain within the area where it was sighted.

Although the whitetail is not a migratory animal, in the popular sense of the word, it may move during the winter months in places of severe weather, to locate available food. However, it will not wander about for long distances, a la the mule deer. Deer sighted in a certain area a week or two prior to the season opening will remain in that area, unless there is a heavy snowfall to move them to more suitable brouse. This latter situation is rare in the fall during the big-game season; it is generally a winter occurrence.

These tests only confirm the beliefs of veteran hunters who have learned the same thing by observation. Take Joe Ralston. He's a confirmed city slicker, having been born, raised and employed in New York City. Yet Joe never misses a deer season. And he's a doggone good hunter, too. He's a firm believer in scouting out an area before hunting it. He says if deer are there before the season, they are going to be there during the season.

Joe told me about a hunt he took a few years ago in Coos County, New Hampshire. A week before the season was to open, he drove over one weekend to look over his prospective hunting site. While he was motoring down a back dirt road, he jumped a deer that ran off a few dozen yards and stopped. Joe braked his car and looked the deer over carefully through binoculars. This was a three-pointer, with the typical forked horn on the left, but the right antler was long and smooth and bent over at a crazy angle.

The season was in its second day before Joe sighted a deer. He jumped a buck from a swath of dense timber flanking a dry creekbed and dropped him with one shot as the deer crossed a clearing.

There was no doubt about this deer. It was the identical three-pointer with the same crooked right antler Joe had sighted just a week earlier. And from the spot where he downed the buck, Joe almost could have thrown a rock and hit the site where he previously had seen the whitetail.

The whitetail may range at times, particularly during the rut and in times of food shortage. Yet its range probably is less than a mile, with the deer habitually returning to its familiar homestead to bed down. I once killed a buck which had corn in his stomach, although the nearest cornfield was almost a mile away. But the deer had returned, undoubtedly, to his regular haunt after eating.

This means, then, that the person who scouts the area he plans on hunting prior to the season opening will be improving considerably his chances of success. This scouting serves a dual purpose. The hunter can search for deer, either by visual sightings or wildlife signs, and look for likely spots to situate his stands or map a pattern to follow while stalk hunting.

Food, of course, will determine the best spots to hunt. Master the food situation and you've taken more than half the guesswork out of deer hunting.

Whitetails feeding along the edges of grassy meadows. When scouting potential deer-hunting areas, look for the regular runs deer use between their feeding and bedding grounds.

A deer must eat, every day. By locating regular runs between feeding and bedding areas, you often can ambush the deer.

The forage of deer will differ with different locales and sections of the country. The New York Conservation Department, in its pamphlet "Food Preferences of the White-Tailed Deer," found that deer in that state ate things like apples, wintergreen, witch bobble, cherry, red maple, basswood, dogwood and staghorn sumac. Beechnuts are a favorite food of deer in New Hampshire. In a study in Missouri it was found that something like 75 per cent of a deer's diet is composed of oaks and acorns. In southern Canada and the far Midwest, various conifers and hardwoods are eaten. Georgia deer feed mainly on oaks.

Farmlands also offer a vital source of deer food and good hunting around agricultural areas is becoming a rule rather than the exception. The reason is obvious. There is a ready-made food supply every year, not just of domestic crops, but also on small woodlots, scrubs and fence rows. When Kent Price bagged his world-record typical whitetail (archery, Pope and Young Club), it wasn't deep in seldom-hunted dense forest, but along a millet and corn field in Maryland. Traditionally, the biggest deer in almost every state come from agricultural areas, due primarily to this bountiful food supply. Farm crop residues which supplement woody plants provide more nourishing food than does overbrowsed woodlands. In fact, crop depredations in many areas have

Saplings that have been partially stripped of their bark by browsing deer are good indicators to look for when scouting before the season opens.

become so acute that the deer are looked upon as pests by the farmers. Nutrition determines the size and numbers of whitetail deer.

The record Missouri deer, weighing 369 pounds on the hoof, came from farm country; and in a comparison made between deer coming from forested counties in Missouri and those from farm country north of the Missouri River it was found that the largest deer, both in weight and antler size, were bagged in the farmlands.

In Mississippi, the biggest deer are found along the Mississippi River, from Tunica County south to Wilkinson County, in the heart of the agriculture belt. The better hunting for whitetails in West Virginia is concentrated through the western counties of Ritchie, Gilmer, Calhoun, Wirt, Jackson and Roane. This is open farm country. In New York, the largest bucks traditionally originate in the agricultural counties of Erie, Mercer, Beaver, Butler and Washington.

Dr. Vagn Flyger of the University of Maryland's Natural Resources Institute made an exhaustive study of deer weights in Maryland, comparing animals taken in the western mountains against those of agricultural Kent County, and he discovered the ones from the latter area were heavier and sported larger antlers than those which browsed solely in the forests.

The idea is to check your locale and find where the deer are feeding. The state game and fish commission is one source of information. Probably a better one is the local game warden or conservation officer. Or maybe farmers and rural mail carriers. Another tip-off is to watch signs along the highway which indicate regular deer crossings.

Once you've pinpointed a general area to hunt, go to the court house for a map of the area. The general topography will give you some inkling as to the best route to follow when hunting. Now, you are ready to go into the area prior to the season opening to scout things out, to get familiar with landmarks and look for deer and deer sign.

Visual sightings are best. When a hunter sees a buck he knows one actually roams the area. It gives him added confidence. But even if he fails to see deer, he can get some inkling as to an area's population from obvious signs such as tracks, droppings and regular runs. One of the better indicators for determining whether or not bucks are present is to look for the rubs where the males have honed and polished their antlers on sapling trees.

Sometimes it is, indeed, difficult actually to see the deer. A man gets more respect for the sagacity of the whitetail when he realizes that even though a deer does live out almost its entire life in such a limited area, there are instances where some old and wise bucks have escaped the wandering horde of hunters for years. In a unique experiment in Michigan a few years back, thirty-four deer were released on a square mile of ordinary forest land surrounded by a deerproof fence. Hunters were then allowed to go into the confines of the square mile of deer habitat. When deer of either sex were legal game, it required fourteen hours of hunting for each deer bagged. For bucks only the ante went up to fifty-one hours of hunting for each deer killed. From this, it is easy to see why killing a deer is no simple feat.

During a pre-season scouting trip, the author searches under the floor of forest leaves for deer tracks along a likely-looking trail. After you have found a good deer area, get a map of the region and study the best routes to take when hunting.

It is this kind of pre-season research and preparation which distinguishes the serious follower of the sport from the beginner or average haphazard hunter. The person who studies the deer and its habits is going to stand the better chance of putting venison on the dinner table, simply because he'll know where to look for deer and can predict what one will do under different circumstances.

This is particularly important for the trophy hunter, the man who seeks a bragging-sized rack of antlers. Big bucks exemplify the survival of the fittest. While their brethren have fallen before hunters' guns, they somehow have survived, and become much wiser to the ways of the human predator. With trophy hunting, a lot depends on hunting where deer with record antlers are known to be. The Boone and Crockett Club chronicles world records for hunting. In thumbing through the club's record book, a person will find that in recent years the best heads have come from Saskatchewan, British Columbia and Manitoba, and the states of Maine, Virginia and Texas.

The skilled deer hunter has studied the everyday habits of deer and often can predict what one will do simply by the way it acts. Every movement a deer makes means something. A deer will, for instance, look at another deer differently from the way it will look at a human. Often, a person who really knows deer behavior can tell, simply by watching a deer's reactions, whether it is alarmed or simply curious about something natural to its environment.

A deer that is looking about occasionally, just idly watching, will hold its ears almost straight up and cupped slightly forward. When alarmed, when listening intently for some danger signal, the ears will stand out at about a forty-five degree angle.

The learned deer hunter also can distinguish between the infrequent sounds which deer make. Almost always the sound will come from a female, the bucks being relatively mute. If it is a low, pleading bleat, the doe probably is communicating with other deer, perhaps a buck that has come courting. But if it is a loud, abrupt snort, she has detected something out of the ordinary and is giving a warning signal.

A snorting doe won't always flee, however. I've had one stand off in the brush and snort loudly over and over again. I stayed put and waited quietly. Soon the deer got over her sudden fright and started feeding again, often wandering out in the open where I could see her.

Yet if there was a buck within hearing distance he likely took off, not

Kent Price with his world-record whitetail, killed with bow and arrow in Maryland farm country. Agricultural regions provide abundant deer food and for that reason often yield better deer hunting than woodlands.

waiting around to determine whether or not it was a false alarm. A buck usually doesn't take the unnecessary chances that a doe does.

Another thing the serious hunter soon learns when studying deer is that tail movements betray what the deer is thinking. If you watch feeding deer for any length of time, you'll observe that each one is glancing up periodically, searching the landscape for anything out of the ordinary. If it twitches its tail back and forth a few times, that means everything is okay and the deer will start feeding again. But if the deer raises its tail it probably means the animal is suspicious.

How far it raises the tail depends on how suspicious it really is. If it throws it straight up, it probably is getting ready to bolt; should it only ease it up halfway it means it is leery, all right, but not quite suspicious enough to run. When you see a deer do this tail raising, be extra cautious to avoid detection, particularly if only does are in sight and you believe a buck might be lingering out of sight in bordering brush. Also watch for the stamping forefoot. A deer that is picking the foot up and dropping it sharply is suspicious of something. When a deer is scared into running, it often will alert every other deer within hearing range.

A doe is much more observant than a buck. Watch deer of both sexes feeding together and you'll note the doe is almost continually raising her head to look around briefly, while the buck seldom raises his. Also notice that, when crossing open places, the buck seldom leads the herd. He lets a doe go first, to determine whether it is safe for him to pass, just as he lets her watch and look while they are feeding.

The hunter also can usually ascertain whether a deer moving through the cover is a doe or buck merely by observing the manner in which it is traveling. A doe tends to run in rapid steps with her head up; the buck keeps his head tucked down, to avoid tangling his antlers in low-hanging limbs and brush, and he takes shorter steps, more of a slip than a run. Of course, the hunter shouldn't shoot at a deer because it *looks* offhand like a buck, but having an idea that it is legal game will aid him in moving around to intercept the retreating deer for a shot.

The idea of studying deer, naturally, is to learn something about their behavior which will give you an advantage when planning your hunt. The deer must be the one that makes the mistakes, not the hunter. It is a battle of wits, in a way, with the hunter's intelligence and reasoning trying to offset the inherent wariness, or woods wisdom, of the whitetail.

As we mentioned earlier, the deer's foremost defensive weapon is its nose. It depends primarily on its use of air currents and smelling ability to detect any enemy. The slightest whiff of human scent is all that is needed to scare one off. When it smells the human it won't be merely suspicious, it will be frightened.

For this reason, contrary to popular belief, it is much better to hunt on a day when there is a light (not strong) prevailing breeze rather than on a still day. By putting the wind to sensible use, the hunter can keep his scent blowing away from the area he hunts. On a still day he may be lured into false security since it doesn't even take a noticeable breeze to carry human scent around. But the hunter must always be on the alert for suddent wind changes which will stymie his strategy.

On still days, the hunter is in a precarious position unless he knows how to counteract the non-movement of air currents. A man who has done extensive experimenting with catfish baits, of all things, proved this. In a still pool of water, the bait lying idle in one spot will give off a scent that slowly seeps outward like concentric circles from a pebble dropped in water. How fast it spreads depends on water temperature. In warm water the scent travels much farther and much faster than it does in colder water. Conversely, the colder the water, the less it travels.

This same pattern holds true with deer hunters and surrounding air. If a hunter is on stand during a warm and still day, his scent will radiate outwards, moving eventually far enough to forewarn any deer that is approaching the hunter's concealed position. (This is important in dense timber and brush when the hunter has a confined field of view.) On a cold day, the scent will move much slower and within a more limited area. It stands to reason, then, that the stand hunter on the calm and warm days must move occasionally, to hold this scent pattern in check. Deer lure, available at most sporting goods stores, sprinkled liberally on the clothing helps mask the strong human odor. The hunter should remain in one place about an hour or two, at the most, on warm days. During colder weather, he might move only every third or fourth hour.

The hunter who makes a serious study of deer behavior is going to be a better hunter than the person who approaches the sport with a haphazard attitude. Learning the habits of deer and how the animals react to various circumstances is the graduate study of deer hunting. The person who takes the time and effort to study his quarry will spend much less time in the woods in relation to the number of deer killed, and in the long run he will bring in much larger deer with bigger antlers than will the person with a lackadaisical approach to the sport.

Every deer hunter dreams of killing a trophy. Because of increased hunting pressure over the years, few bucks live to a ripe old age anymore. Standards are high and record-book kills are rare. But a few still are made each season.

The Boone and Crockett Club was established in 1949 to compile world-record hunting trophies. The present record typical whitetail, measured in 1960 but killed in 1918, was taken near Funkley, Minnesota, and scored 202 points. A set of typical antlers must score at least 150 to make the record list published by Boone and Crockett while the minimum score for a non-typical head is 140:20 or 160 points.

A trophy head can not be measured until 60 days after it is killed, to allow for shrinkage. A typical head, basically, is one that scores about the same on both sides and has the symmetrical balance of the classic whitetail head. Many whitetails, no matter how old they may be, will have no more than ten points, four on either side and two brow points. Should a set of antlers have four points on one side and only three on the other, this would not make it non-typical. This wouldn't be freakish since the animal simply failed to grow the extra matching point. The head would be graded as typical, but the head would lose credit due to unbalance or non-symmetry.

In a typical head, all points grow off the main beams. When another point forks from a typical point, this is abnormal. Also, if a head has two brow points on one side it is freakish. When the score of a non-typical head is entered in the record books, it will be a compound score such as $187\frac{1}{4}:25\frac{1}{4}$ or $212\frac{1}{2}$ total points. The second number indicates the length of abnormal points while the first is the score of the typical version of the antlers. The second number may be a conclusive determining factor as to whether or not the head makes it into the record book. There is a world-record non-typical whitetail head on display in the Lone Star Brewing Company at San Antonio, Texas, which scored $149:137=286$. That deer was shot in McCulloch County in central Texas. It was killed in 1892.

Most taxidermists know enough about Boone and Crockett measurements to give you some idea whether you should write for an official entry blank and find the whereabouts of the nearest official measuring representative. An entry blank can be obtained by writing the Boone and Crockett Club, 5 Tudor City Place, New York, N.Y.

The Pope and Young Club was established in 1957 to give credit to bowhunters, setting up a record list similar to that of the Boone and Crockett Club, but with lower standards since the archer obviously can't compete with riflemen. A typical whitetail must score 115 and a non-typical $105 + 15$ to qualify for the Pope and Young list. An official entry blank is available from the Pope and Young Club, Box 887, Des Moines, Washington.

12 Bow Hunting

I'VE BEEN in close proximity with whitetail deer all my life. I was raised in the heart of Texas' finest deer country. My current home is surrounded by prime deer habitat. My first deer was killed when I was nine years old and I've missed very few seasons since without getting at least one deer.

That's why I unhesitantly accepted a challenge from a friend of mine to try bow hunting. I reasoned that I knew deer behavior well enough to get close enough to bag one of the critters easily with this, the most primitive of all weapons.

I wasn't naive enough to believe I could go out during the peak of the rifle season and expect to get a buck with bow-and-arrow. But I got a permit for an antlerless deer, a doe, and figured I could at least kill one of the less suspicious females.

Was I in for a rude awakening! I'll never forget my first shot at a deer with a hunting bow. I doubt whether I did anything right. The doe came tiptoeing down the game trail, across a small clearing from where I crouched in hiding behind a makeshift blind of cut bushes. Instead of shooting from the downed position, I tried to rise up and draw the 51-pound Bear bow. The deer glimpsed the movement and bolted. I fired hastily and the arrow whished harmlessly over her back.

When I trudged campward that evening I was a frustrated and exasperated hunter. Three chances I'd gotten and three times I'd fouled things up royally. Mentally I was exhausted. I'd been too tense and too keyed up all day to relax. My nerve ends were rubbed raw.

But there was one consolation. I'd gained a new-found respect for the bow hunter. This, I decided, is the ultimate in deer hunting, the true challenge. While I'm not planning to discard my trusty rifle for the bow, I'm still fascinated by bow hunting and usually I try my success with the Indian weapon at least once or twice every season.

Bow hunting has really boomed in recent years. No longer is the hand-drawn weapon looked upon as a child's toy. In the hands of a proficient shooter, it is a deadly weapon, indeed, and a challenging one.

Nowadays, the bow hunter enjoys the privilege of special deer season in most every state. This special season is necessary since the bow-and-arrow enthusiast can't hope to compete on equal terms with the rifle shooter. During the regular deer season the animals become spooky and wild and the bow hunter has all the odds stacked against him.

Just being a proficient shot is no assurance of killing a deer. In fact, most bowmen I've talked with agree that it is much more important to be an exceptional hunter than it is a marksman shot. Nationwide statistics reveal that the average deer bagged with a bow is taken at a range of slightly less than thirty yards. No wonder the bowman has to be an extraordinary hunter.

The bow hunter today is armed with the finest equipment in the history of bow-and-arrow hunting. It is true quality, and the many diversified accessories add to the enjoyment and productivity of the sport. The modern bow hunter can sleeve his hunting bow with camouflage-colored cloth, can use special attachments to nock his arrow at the same spot on the bowstring each time, and quieteners which take the twang out of the released string, to keep from spooking deer.

The prospective bow hunter, shopping around for a basic beginning outfit, should consult someone familiar with the sport in selecting his equipment. Few sporting goods dealers have this knowledge. The bow hunter who has mismatched equipment already has two strikes against him, before he ever steps into the woods.

The hunter should select the type of bow and the weight which suits him best. The most popular bow is one that is recurved, constructed from a wood core with laminated fiberglass covering. The weight of the bow (amount of pull in pounds needed to bring it to full draw position) depends on the hunter's physical capabilities. He should be able to draw the bow to full position, the entire length of the arrow, easily without excessive strain. All shots are taken from the full-draw position and having a bow that is too strenuous to pull will keep a person from developing proper shooting technique.

Many hunters have the misconception that a bow pulling at least fifty pounds of weight is necessary in killing deer. They buy the heavier bows and wonder why they never become proficient shots. Actually, a bow pulling forty pounds is adequate for deer. In Wisconsin, for example, the legal limit size on deer-hunting bows is thirty pounds.

The hunter also must obtain arrows matched to the specific bow he buys. And every arrow should be of the same length and weight to give comparable performance with each shot. Arrows come in many materials—wood, aluminum and fiberglass, with the latter two being most expensive and durable.

Two essential items of the bowman are a leather armguard, which fits on the inside of the bow arm, and a shooting glove that covers the first three fingers of the shooting hand, the three fingers which grip the bow string. The glove protects these fingers against blisters as the string rubs over them on

Two methods of stringing a bow. At left, the archer braces one end against his instep, pulling toward him with his right hand and pushing away with his left hand, which slides bowstring into place. At right, he uses his right leg as a fulcrum to bend the bow into position with both hands at the end.

Orthodox stance for bow shooting—feet placed comfortably apart, the left foot slightly advanced, with both feet at right angles to an imaginery line toward the target. Bow is slightly canted to the right at full draw position.

release, and the armguard keeps the string from slapping the tender inside of the arm.

The fundamentals of bow shooting are stance, draw, anchor, hold, aim, release and follow through. The orthodox shooting position is both feet spread comfortably apart, the left foot (if you are right handed) slightly advanced, with both feet at right angles on an imaginary line extending from

At full draw position, the arrow should be anchored against the face—at the same point for every shot. Arrow should always be pulled to its full length.

Release is accomplished smoothly by allowing the string to roll away from the fingers naturally, keeping the line of sight always on the target.

Quick method of checking suitable arrow length is to put one end against your chest and extend hands to tip. Ideally, the arrow should be exactly the length from the chest to the tip of the fingers.

bowman to target. The bow is slightly canted to the right at full draw position to bring the arrow into best position for sighting.

The bow is drawn evenly and smoothly to full position, the length of the arrow. The anchor is a position alongside the face where the arrow is drawn to each time, to assure a comparable release with each successive shot. The hold is the time the archer has the bow at full draw. It is an integral fundamental since the tendency is to pull back, aim and release in one continuous motion, which cuts down on overall accuracy. It is better to go to a lighter weight bow which the shooter can keep control of at the full position. With a bow of excessive weight he will start wavering off balance, unable to keep a steady aim. Aiming is, more than anything, concentration. The shooter should aim with both eyes open, superimposing the arrow on the target, the very spot he wishes to hit on a deer. With the anchor he should bring the bow back alongside the face, in instinctive shooting, to a point best suited to the individual shooter. It might be at the chin or just under the mouth. The release should be so the string simply rolls smoothly off the three fingers holding it. In the follow through, the hold should remain at full-draw position as long as the arrow remains in contact with the bow. To relax arm muscles the instant the fingers release the string will throw the arrow off true aim.

The bowman must practice long and assiduously to master good shooting form. Unlike the rifleman, who can accomplish fairly accurate shooting in one afternoon of basic practice, the bow hunter needs weeks to become proficient with his weapon.

Hunting arrows are tipped either with two- or three-bladed broadheads or four-bladed razorheads. Unlike the rifle bullet, an arrow kills by hemorrhage rather than shock. The best spots to aim for are either the chest cavity when the deer is facing head on, or behind the foreshoulder about a third of the way up, when it is broadside. An arrow in either of these vital areas will sever the most blood vessels, hit the lungs, and cause excessive bleeding. Often an arrow will pass completely through the animal if it doesn't hit an obstruction, like the shoulder bone.

Because of the very nature of the arrow hit, sans the shock, the deer usually is unaware that whatever injured it is anywhere close about. If the hunter allows it time, the deer will lie down and soon bleed to death. Normally, a hit deer that is not pursued will lie down within 200 feet. The hunter should give it at least thirty minutes to succumb.

Another selling point on bow hunting is that deer crippled with arrows are much less likely to die than are those wounded with bullets, simply because the shock hasn't ruptured vital vessels which is almost certain to bring eventual death.

Most bow hunters favor quivers which attach either to the bow or belt. The time-honored back quiver is not as evident in the woods anymore. Arrows in a quiver of this type tend to make too much noise, hang on brush and there is too much movement when reaching for an arrow.

Camouflage clothing is a standard item among bow hunters. Attire of this type causes the hunter to blend with the background. Some bowmen even go

Camouflage clothing is standard garb for the bow hunter, who must be able to stalk within thirty yards of his quarry for a killing shot.

as far to cover their bows, hands and faces with netlike camouflage material. Some supplement this with portable blinds made from camouflage-colored tarpaulin.

Commercial scents also are widely accepted among bow hunters. Although a few manufacturers advertise their products as "buck lures," the scent doesn't actually attract deer but merely aids in submerging the human odors. Most bowmen I've talked with swear by the scents, sprinkling the liquid liberally on their clothing before heading afield. One told me he approached a deer from upwind last season and the deer actually failed to detect him because of his wise use of scents.

Since bow hunters need their quarry to be much closer than does the rifleman, the problem of radiating human odors on still days, as mentioned in the previous chapter, is much more pronounced in bow hunting. The scents are designed to eliminate much of this handicap.

The bow hunter must be versatile. He either seeks deer off a stand or by still hunting, stalking through the woods on silent feet. He must be able to get off quick shots in contorted positions—and usually he'll be firing while on his knees—or by swinging around rather than in the orthodox target-shooting stance. Being able to send that first arrow winging on a true course is all important since there might not be the opportunity for a second chance.

A person, if he so chooses, can hunt both during the special archery season

Commercial scent is used by most bow hunters to submerge human odors. It is sprinkled liberally on clothing, aids in approaching deer within bow-and-arrow range.

Skilled stalking and accurate shooting are essential to the bow hunter. This archer has managed to approach a deer close enough to warrant a shot—and the first one really counts.

and the regular gun season in most states, although his season bag limit of deer will be the same as for a hunter enjoying only one of the seasons. If he succeeds during the archery shoot, he is through for the year; but should he fail to get his deer, he can bring out the trusty rifle and try again, after the archery season.

Hunting deer with bow and arrow dates back to the Indians, but it really didn't enjoy any real growth in this country until the past two decades. Two factors, more than anything else, have been an impetus to this phenomenal boom in bow hunting. One is the superior equipment; the other, the special bow seasons. The archer simply can't compete with the rifle hunter on equal terms. Once an animal is spooked by gunshot, seldom can the bow hunter stalk close enough for a chance with his arrow.

Bow hunting was a real novelty back in 1923 when Dr. Saxton Pope wrote his book called *Hunting With Bow and Arrow*. But his writings, along with those of his hunting companion Art Young, kindled an interest in the sport, and by the 1930s hunters were beginning to take to the woods with bows and arrows in hand. Finally, in 1934, interest reached the point where Wisconsin decided to open a special archery deer season, to find whether it would work and whether there were enough bow hunters to support it. Michigan followed suit in 1937, and 186 hunters turned out for the first archery season. Nowadays all states which have deer seasons have special archery seasons, and usually the seasons are quite liberal in length. Bow-hunting pressure, it has been found, causes only negligible inroads in deer population. Overall hunter success is less than 10 per cent.

In bow hunting the kill isn't what is important. The appeal of the sport is the challenge involved. Should you just get close enough for a reasonable shot at a deer with a bow, you can figure that your season has been fairly successful. Approach upon a deer within thirty yards or less is quite a feat, and actually killing one of the wary animals is even more remarkable. It is something every successful bow hunter can be quite proud of.

13 Hit or Miss

A MAJORITY of the hunters who shoot at deer and then see the animals run off assume their shots were misses. Untold hundreds of deer are left to rot in the woods each year for this reason. The hunter doesn't take the time or make the effort to find out that his shot actually was a miss.

Sometimes, a deer will be knocked over as if pole-axed when struck by a high-velocity bullet. Other times, it will hunch or jump if hit. But I've seen deer that were hit solidly in a vital area bolt off spiritedly as if they'd never been touched.

I was once hunting with a friend who fired at a deer and swore 'til the earth looked level that he'd missed the deer cleanly. I insisted we go look, to be positive. That buck, struck squarely through the heart, had run less than one hundred feet before folding.

Occasionally, a bullet placed in the deer's most vital organ, its heart, won't bring instant death. Of course it is eventually fatal, but the deer may run for considerable distance, carried along only by a spurt of adrenalin. The more frightened a deer is before hit, the farther the boost of adrenalin will carry it. This might be 200 yards or farther.

A bullet which sails just a mite off its aimed mark may inflict only a wound which goes undetected offhand by the hunter. But by checking, the nimrod can satisfy himself whether or not it was a hit or miss. There may not be any telltale blood, but there is one visible sign a struck deer always leaves behind, hair. When a high-velocity bullet strikes an animal it is going to blast loose some hair, the amount depending on the exact location of the hit.

There are too many intangibles involved in hunting to assure an instant kill every time. The hunter shooting from a draw up an incline, like a hill for example, tends to undershoot, unless he compensates by aiming higher on the animal, while the person firing from an elevated position, such as the top of a hill, down into a draw, will often overshoot unless he aims low. The hunter pulling down on a running deer might hit the animal too far back for a quick kill. A deer standing at an angle to the hunter may receive only a glancing shot that perhaps cuts through the flesh of the hindquarter without striking bone. A deer so hit might run for a long way, but often the painstaking hunter can follow the spoor until he either jumps the animal again for a finishing-off shot or finds it dead.

I witnessed a remarkable trailing job by Miles Bingaman, a deer-hunting veteran with wide experience, on a ranch in south Texas a few seasons back. One of the hunters on the Diamond H near Catarina had crippled a deer. The only spoor was scattered droplets of blood. Bingaman started unraveling the trail, combing the ground with infinite care, sometimes going for yards between tiny pin-top drips of blood. Every time he'd lose the trail momentarily, he'd mark the last spot he had discovered blood and start circling, each time around gradually increasing the size of his circle until he scouted the territory for dozens of yards in each direction. He'd eventually pick up the trail again. After more than three hours and many miles, he finally came to the animal, down but still alive, too sick to continue farther.

In some Texas counties, dogs are permitted by law to be used in trailing crippled deer. If there is any fresh blood at all, a trained dog will quickly run down the wounded deer. Dogs prevent loss of many cripples, but the anti-dog faction says there is too great a tendency for the canines to chase and kill healthy deer, by getting off the original trail and onto the track of another animal which just happened to pass in the same vicinity. Most persons experienced in the use of trained dogs for trailing wounded deer say this is fallacy. Very seldom will a dog get off the track of a crippled animal to chase one that is healthy and spry, they tell me.

If a deer is hit solidly in a vital area, there probably will be a very distinguishable blood trail to follow. But let the bullet strike in some place like the hip bone or low paunch and the animal might not bleed at all immediately. Often a deer so hit will run quite a ways from the original spot where it was hit before beginning to bleed.

A hunter came in to the landowner's house on a ranch he was hunting last season and announced that he had wounded a deer, but he couldn't find anything but some scattered hair, no blood. I was visiting with the rancher at the time, so I accompanied him to look-see around the vicinity. We found the spot where the deer was standing when hit, all right, and tracks where it had crashed off into the brush. Painstakingly we followed the tracks. Perhaps one hundred feet farther we came to a pool of blood which appeared as if it had been poured from a bucket. Evidently the deer had paused momentarily and the blood started flowing freely. Not fifty yards farther along we discovered the deer dead, piled up in a clump of brush where it had lay down.

The hunter should never take anything for granted when he shoots at a deer. He should always check to make sure he actually missed. Sometimes the deer might be dead nearby, or crippled.

If there is evidence of blood, the wounded animal should be allowed time to lie down and succumb. About thirty minutes is sufficient. When trailing, always look ahead periodically to try and glimpse the animal lying down or sneaking away. Usually the tracker can walk right up on a sick deer before it attempts to struggle away.

Every hunter owes it to himself and his fellow hunters to exert every effort to finding deer he may have crippled. Leaving a deer to rot needlessly in the woods is, in my opinion, the most loathsome sin a hunter can commit.

14 Field-Dressing and Butchering the Deer Carcass

WE'LL ASSUME you have a deer down in the woods. It is an exhilarating moment, the climax of a long and tedious search, the legendary pot of gold at the end of the rainbow. But it is no time to let excitement overwhelm common sense. That deer lying there innocently may be potential danger, if he isn't completely dead. Always approach a downed animal with respect from behind. Punch him with your gun barrel in an attempt to detect any flickering sign of life.

Whenever I approach a downed deer, I recall something that happened to a friend of mine, one Buzzy Keller. He walked up to a fallen animal which he assumed was dead, straddled over the buck and started to dress him out. Unexpectedly, the deer came to life and started struggling frantically, trying to free himself from the hunter, shaking his antlered head and flailing his sharp hoofs. Buzzy held on desperately with his left hand and with his right hand punched at the deer with his knife. Fortunately, he killed the deer, but not until he was skinned and bruised and given quite a scare.

After the deer is dead and harmless, then comes the routine labor of any successful hunt. The deer must be field-dressed immediately to assure prime steaks and chops on the dinner platter. The taint of the meat is particularly evident when the innards of the deer have been shot and the animal isn't gutted right away.

A handy item for any hunter to carry is a short length of rope to tie a hindleg to one side making dressing easier, or maybe two ropes to spread both legs. Otherwise, just turn the animal on its back and prop with logs or rocks, anything to steady it.

I first cut away the pads on the inside of either hindleg. This isn't absolutely a must, but the pads of a buck possess a foul odor.

Then I insert the blade of a sharp knife just in front of the genitals and cut back to the anus. Reversing the blade, I go forward, slitting the abdomen from aitchbone to breastbone. If the head is to be mounted, stop the

Always approach a downed deer with caution. Come up slowly and wait a few feet away for a minute or two to see if there is any movement.

incision before you reach the forequarters, to assure a handsome cape. Otherwise, go on forward, past the breastbone and up the neck. Position yourself behind the deer so that you cut forward, as a safety precaution should the blade slip.

Gently squeeze on the bladder, if it is full, to free its contents, cut around the anus to clear the intestines from the pelvic arch or aitchbone, where the hipbones are connected. Draw the intestines into the body cavity. Inside the abdomen, at the breastbone, cut the membrane which holds the innards to the deer, being particularly careful not to sever the stomach or intestines. Just below the head, cut the windpipe and esophagus, and with both hands pull them downward until everything is free to the mid-section. Now you can turn the deer over and shake the innards out. Just prior to this last step, remove the heart and liver if you wish to save them. The smart hunter carries

If the animal is not dead it can inflict serious injury with its antlers or hoofs. Poke him with your gun barrel to detect any sign of life.

a large and stout plastic bag in his hip pocket for carrying the liver and heart back to camp. If two men are packing out the deer on a pole, the heart and liver can be carried inside the body cavity.

If it is seasonably warm weather the deer should be taken immediately to a locker or cold-storage plant. This may be impossible at times, however. Should the nights be cold and the days warm, it is imperative to capture and hold as much of the chill as possible. Skin the deer promptly. The hide acts as insulation and prevents the meat from cooling properly. Prop the carcass open with a stick where air can circulate inside. After it cools at night, cover with a light mesh deer bag to protect the carcass from flies. Hang it in a cool, shady spot. Swab the inside with a damp cloth and remove as much of the bullet-damaged flesh as possible.

One way to keep the carcass cool during the day is to put your sleeping

Deer can be hauled out of the woods in tandem by roping them to a branch with a hunter carrying each end.

bag around it and zip it snug. The insulation captures the coolness and holds it inside. But first wrap the deer with some sort of cloth, to keep blood from dripping inside your sleeping bag. Remove the bag at night (naturally you'll need it to sleep in) and let the carcass chill down again.

Although the universal method of skinning a deer is to hang it by its hindlegs, I prefer to do just the opposite, to tie the animal up by its neck or antlers. This way the hide slips down with the grain of the meat and under-lying fat. If you're going to mount the head, hanging by the hindquarters has an obvious advantage since you can slip the hide completely to the head before severing the neck.

When hanging by its neck or antlers, cut an incision around the deer's throat, just below the head, and start peeling the skin downward. With the alternate method, cut around each hind leg just below the hocks and start pulling the hide off, using your knife whenever flesh starts to give with the

One of the best ways to get deer out of rough country is to tie the animal's feet over a pole, which is carried on hunters' shoulders.

skin. After the rear legs are skinned, cut the tail at the base and strip the hide off the body down to the shoulders. Skin the front legs, peel the hide to the base of the neck. Remove the feet by cutting the flesh and tendons at the knee joints and bend each leg back sharply until the joint snaps. Sever the neck tendons and twist the head off. If you've hung the animal by the neck to skin, you'll have to rehang by the rear legs for cooling. This is done by splitting the membrane under the tendons of the hindlegs, inserting a gambrel stick to spread the hindquarters, and hanging from the garage rafters or a tree limb.

Most hunters simply drape their deer on the hoods of their autos, or the front bumpers, and head homeward. On long trips, this is the worst possible thing to do. Engine heat soon transfers to the animals and spoilage comes quickly. Probably the best spot for transporting the deer is on the auto's top. This is where a station wagon rack comes in handy. Otherwise, carry the deer in the car's storage trunk. If the weather is warm, get a bag of crushed ice at the first stop and lay it inside the carcass. This will keep it cool. Another method is to wrap the carcass in a heavy piece of tarp. This insulates the coolness inside.

When transporting your deer by car, tie the carcass across the rear deck of the automobile or place it in the trunk. Keep it away from heat of the engine.

If you're on a lengthy trip and stop for the night, remember to lift the trunk lid and allow the animal to cool during the night. Heat from the road and automobile collects in the trunk. It is even better to remove the animal completely and hang it up, propped open, and allow it to cool thoroughly. When in doubt, always use ice liberally to keep the animal chilled.

Many hunters simply carry their deer to a local processing plant where, for a nominal fee, they can have it skinned, butchered and wrapped for the deepfreeze. But butchering a deer carcass is a do-it-yourself process that is fairly easy if you follow a routine.

First divide the carcass into equal halves by sawing through the center of the backbone. To quarter, cut each half in two by slicing between the last rib and the one forward. Most hunters make the mistake of making the wrong cut here, dividing the half behind the last rib.

Lay the hindquarter on a sturdy support, perhaps on an old bedsheet spread on the garage floor. Trim away meat on the leg bone and cut away the flank, placing this miscellaneous meat in a pan to be later ground into hamburger and chili meat. Position the ham so that the leg bone extends off to the right. Cut diagonally at upper end of ham to remove the triangular chunk which is the rump roast. Then slice round steaks to the thickness desired. The lower end of the ham, near the leg bone, can be cut into steaks or left intact as a heel roast.

Separate the shoulder from the loin section by cutting between the fifth and sixth ribs. Divide the tenderloin and ribs by cutting horizontally just three or four inches below the spine. The tenderloin then can be sliced into

If you carry your deer in the car's trunk and stop overnight, it is best to remove the animal, hang it up, and prop it open to allow it to cool thoroughly.

steaks, cutting vertically to desired thickness, by using knife and saw. The ribs can be divided into rib steaks, left intact for barbecuing, or the meat can be trimmed off for use in hamburger and chili meat. The rib section can be divided horizontally to make short or spare ribs.

Separate the neck from the shoulder just forward of the shoulder bone. The neck can be cut into pot roasts, chunked into stew meat or used in hamburger and chili preparations. Cut the leg off and divide the shoulder in half, about halfway down, at the shoulder joint. The upper half of the shoulder makes a nice roast, while the lower half can be sliced into shoulder steaks, utilized as a roast, or ground.

HOW TO FIELD DRESS YOUR DEER

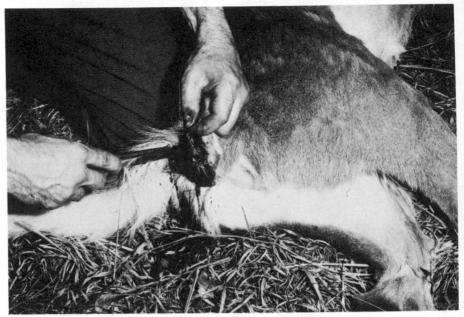

1. Start by cutting close circle around anus and connecting alimentary canal. Make cut as deep as knife will reach.

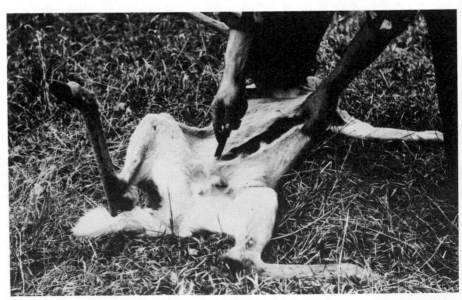

2. Open belly as shown, being careful not to cut intestines. Fork the incision to pass on either side of sex organs.

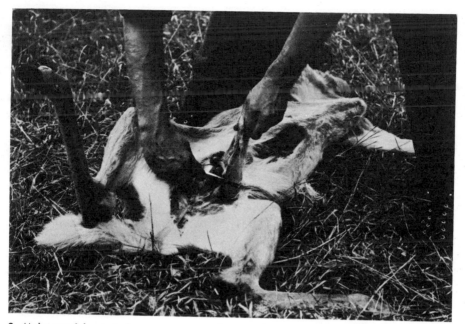

3. Make careful cuts to loosen scrotum and penis. Then pull detached anus and alimentary canal through pelvic arch.

4. Break membrane over chest cavity and reach far up to cut the windpipe loose. Pull out all the organs and entrails.

5. Put heart and liver in a bloodproof plastic bag that will keep both meat and clothes clean.

6. Tip the carcass as shown and drain out blood collected inside. Wipe body cavity dry with cloth or dead grass.

7. Prop body cavity open with stick to let in cooling air. Hang carcass unless you plan to pack it out immediately.

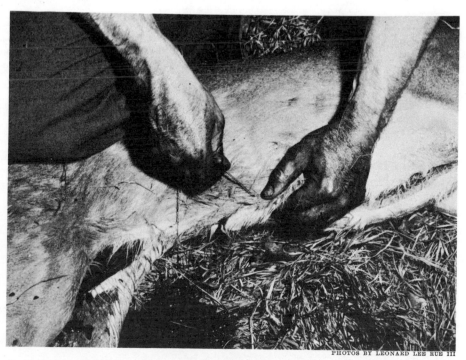

8. To protect your clothes, sew up deer you plan to back-pack out of the woods. Body cavity is spread open again when you get the deer to car or camp.

109

9. Cut off the hair-tufted glands on hind legs. Some say they taint meat.

10. At home or base camp, hang deer by neck or antlers for skinning.

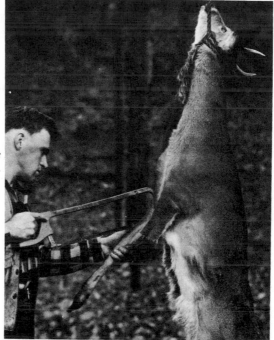

11. Saw or knife off all four legs at center joints. Lower legs are waste.

12. Slit skin on inside of the four legs down to belly cut.

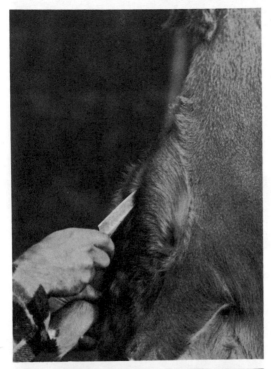

13. Extend belly cut up brisket and throat, splitting the breastbone.

14. Cut around neck. If head is to be mounted, cut lower than shown.

15. Pull skin on down, using knife as needed to work hide loose.

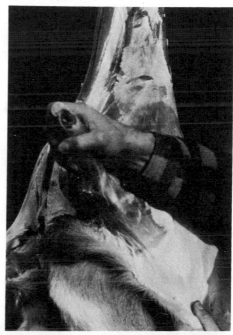

16. Hide will pull off like a stubborn banana peel. Knife is used only in the tight spots.

PHOTOS BY LEONARD LEE RUE III

HOW TO BUTCHER YOUR DEER

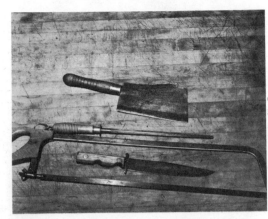

1. These are the tools needed to do quick and easy job of cutting up a skinned carcass: cleaver, sharpening steel, knife, and meat saw.

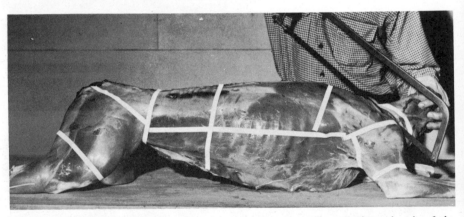

2. Tape on the skinned deer marks out the 11 major cuts used to divide each side of the carcass. Start with neck cut.

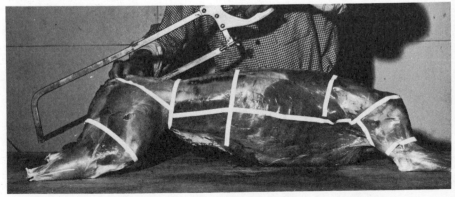

3. Toughest cut to make is long one down the backbone, shown above. It helps to have assistant to steady carcass at this point.

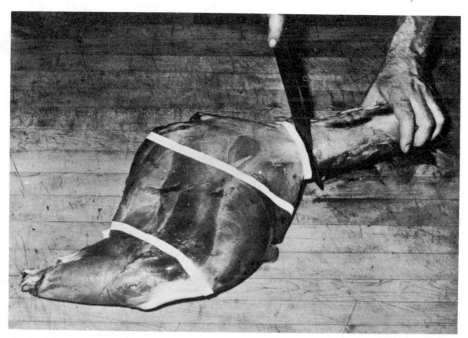

4. Flank has been cut off to be chopped up for deerburger. Knife cut being made here will lop off the loin portion.

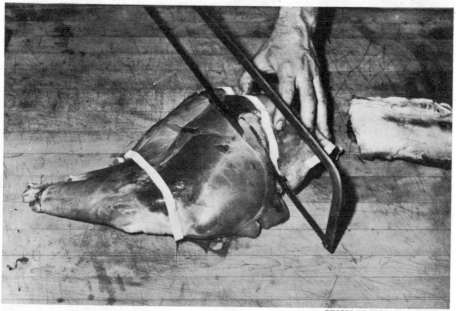

5. Sharp knife makes cuts to bone, which is severed with saw. Hand holds rump roast. Round steaks coming up.

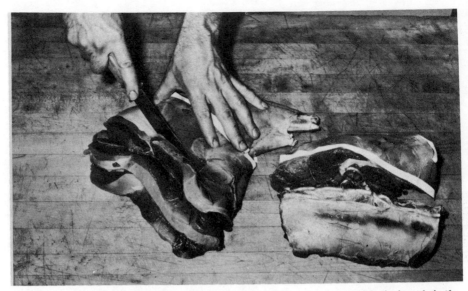

6. Round-steak portion should be divided into even slices about one inch thick with knife. Saw cuts center bone.

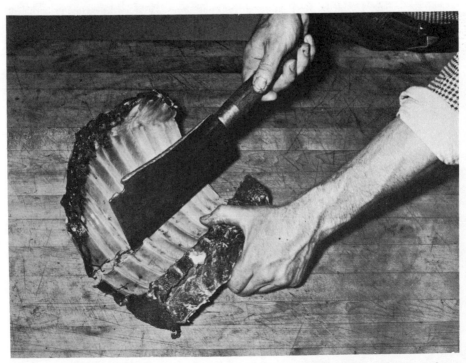

7. Left hand holds the rib-chop section while cleaver lops off lower ribs. Cleaver is faster than saw for this cut.

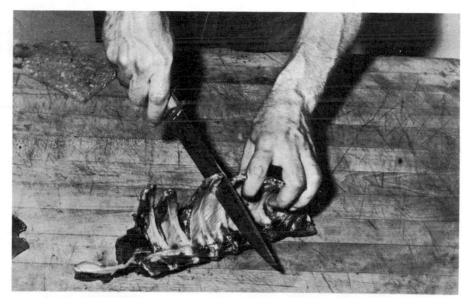

8. Knife cuts divide rib chops. Cleaver will clip the bone portion. Some leave this piece intact for rib roast.

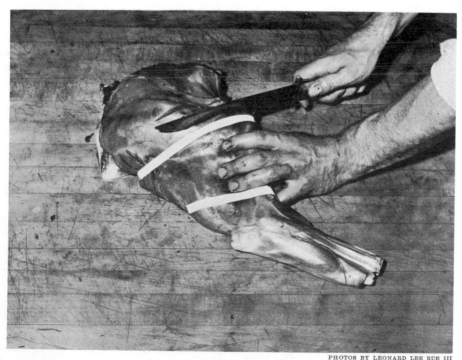

9. Working up fore shoulder. The two tape-marked cuts at top make roasts. Shank is cut up for deerburger.

10. Round steaks are wrapped in aluminum foil for freezer storage. Use large sheets that cover meat completely.

11. Cover foil-wrapped venison with airtight plastic bags tied securely. Frozen, the meat keeps indefinitely.

15 Preserving the Trophy

A TAXIDERMIST once told me that three-fourths of the deer heads brought to him for mounting were in pretty sad shape. To get a respectable product requires painstaking hours of patching and shaping. Even then, the finished product isn't up to the quality of a head which is handled properly *before* it reaches the taxidermist.

When a hunter gets that once-in-a-lifetime rack of antlers, naturally he wants the head preserved for posterity. If his mount isn't near-perfect, he blames the taxidermist. Yet usually the blame rests on his own shoulders.

The first thing to remember is never, under any circumstance, cut the throat of a deer which you intend to have mounted. A cut throat will be the most obvious spot on a mounted head and is almost impossible to repair so that it isn't noticeable.

The ideal arrangement, when possible, is to rush the skin and head to the taxidermist promptly after skinning the deer. Or perhaps the head can be frozen, later to be carried to the taxidermist, leaving the tedious skinning of the head to him. When the carcass is separated from the head, preserve the entire skin and head. Don't attempt to cape the animal yourself. The experienced taxidermist is the best judge of how much body hide is to be utilized on the mount.

If the head and hide can't be frozen, they will soon spoil, ruining the precious trophy. In this case the hunter must skin out the head himself. This is no hurry-up job; rather, the hunter should be meticulous and painstaking to assure that he doesn't damage the head in any way.

Starting below the shoulders on the back, make an incision up the neck to a point about four inches below the antlers. Insert the knife blade at the bottom and cut up, slicing evenly so the hide will be divided but the hair won't be harmed. This way the incision can be sewed together later without being noticeable.

Cut away excessive hide beyond the shoulders, leaving only the head, neck and shoulders. Leave more than enough hide so there will be ample to make a handsome cape. Now make a Y-shaped cut from the top of the incision at the base of the skull up to either antler.

Skin out the neck until you reach the ears, cut through the cartilage close to the skull and free the ears. Continue upwards until you reach near the antlers, being extra cautious to avoid cutting the skin. Insert the knife point down alongside each antler and gradually work the hide loose. Don't attempt to come up entirely to the antlers from the bottom since this tends to remove all the antler hair.

Skin the top of the head over and down to the eyes. Skinning around the eyes is a delicate operation. Proceed slowly and carefully to avoid damaging the skin, particularly where the hide is attached to bone at the eye corners.

Gently peel the skin on down to the mouth and nostrils. Here is another critical point. Carefully cut the lips loose inside the mouth, including the skin of the inside lips since it is necessary for the mounting process.

Now that the skin is freed from the skull, lay it out on a flat surface and flesh it thoroughly, cutting away excessive fat and flesh from around the inside lips, nostrils and eyes, avoiding any unnecessary cuts that may damage the skin.

If you are unable to keep the skin stored in a cool place, or it will be several days before you can get it to the taxidermist, the ears must be skinned out to avoid spoilage. Begin at the ear base and separate the back skin from the cartilage, gradually forcing a blunt instrument between the two. Turn the ear completely inside out. The cartilage must only be divided from the back of the ear, leaving it attached to the inside of the front skin as some taxidermists use it in rebuilding the ear. Use due caution to avoid cutting the skin.

After the skin has been carefully fleshed, cover with salt and rub it in vigorously. It is impossible to over-salt the skin, so be liberal. Afterwards, fold the salted hide, flesh sides together, roll up and bind tightly and place in a cool, preferably dark spot for about twenty-four hours. Untie, lay open and allow to dry. Be sure it is flat so the skin doesn't dry in folds, causing the hair to slip.

Remove the antlers from the head by sawing away the skull just beneath the base of the antlers, leaving the antlers on a cupped plate. Flesh away all excess meat.

This may seem like unnecessarily painstaking work, but the proper care and handling of a trophy, before it reaches the taxidermist, can not be overemphasized. In the long run, it will assure a more handsome and striking mount, one that the hunter can be proud to show to his friends.

16 Preparing and Cooking Venison

I ONCE had a business acquaintance who claimed he couldn't stomach the taste of wild meat, like venison. He said the gamy taste was repulsive. He didn't know it at the time, but he was to be the unsuspecting guinea pig in a self-styled scientific experiment of mine. The "laboratory" was a backyard barbecue grill. The ingredients were venison steaks, cut to a thickness of one-and-one-half inches, a homemade barbecue sauce, some charcoal brickets and hickory chips.

After an elaborate dinner, highlighted by reddish-colored venison cooked medium done, the man commented that he'd never tasted such delicious steaks. I didn't let him know differently, allowing him to go his merry way, still holding to his firm convictions, but I'd satisfied my own curiosity. Venison can, if prepared and cooked correctly, be a gourmet's delight.

Me, I like the wild taste of venison. If I prefer steak, I can get it at the corner supermarket cheaper and easier than I can by deer hunting. One of the real bonuses of deer hunting, as far as I'm concerned, is the later treat on the dinner table.

But getting back to our venison hater. We fooled him by concocting a preparation containing one quart of water, two tablespoons of vinegar and a level teaspoon of household soda. The venison steaks were saturated in the liquid for thirty minutes, removed and drained on paper towels. Then they were barbecued.

The vinegar tends to "draw" the wild taste out of venison, but you must watch and not oversoak since the venison can acquire a vinegar flavor if left in the preparation too long. The soda acts as a tenderizer. Some people substitute a quart of sweet milk for the water-vinegar mixture, with the same effect.

My barbecue sauce is prepared by melting three sticks of margarine in a saucepan and adding one-half teaspoon of Worcestershire sauce, one eight-ounce can of tomato sauce or one cup of catsup, one teaspoon of black pepper, one teaspoon of salt, one-half cup of chopped onion, one-half cup lemon juice, one-half teaspoon oregano, one-half teaspoon garlic salt, one-half teaspoon of rosemary, and one-half teaspoon thyme.

Unlike steak, venison should be turned regularly, about every ten minutes, and basted liberally with the sauce. The margarine keeps the dry venison from becoming tough and juiceless, and the sauce forms a crisp crust on the meat. Or if you prefer, the venison can be marinated in the sauce for three to four hours before cooking.

Another way of improving venison for cooking, particularly roasts, is to trim away the tissue-thin membrane which covers the meat. Removal of this membrane allows juices to penetrate the meat more readily and makes it more tender.

Here are some other favorite venison dishes:

Broiled venison: Take venison steaks cut to desired thickness and rub with a split clove of garlic. Cook about four inches from heat, either on outdoor grill or indoor range, basting with melted margarine or butter. After the meat has seared, to hold the juices in, salt and pepper to taste. Don't overcook. Remove from fire when just a hint of red remains in the heart of the steak.

Venison stew: Cut two pounds of venison into one-inch cubes. Brown the venison in frying pan containing one tablespoon of shortening. Place in pan with four cups of boiling water, one teaspoon Worcestershire sauce, one medium cubed onion, one clove of garlic chopped, one tablespoon salt and one-half teaspoon black pepper. Allow to simmer until venison is tender. Add three medium potatoes cut into chunks, one cup of frozen peas and one cup frozen carrots. Continue cooking until vegetables are done and mixture thickens.

Venison cutlets: Two pounds of cutlets. Roll in mixture containing one cup flour, one-half cup milk, two tablespoons water, two slightly beaten eggs, six tablespoons fat, dash of Worcestershire sauce, dash of celery salt, salt and pepper. Fry over medium heat.

Venison roast: Brown meat slowly on all sides. Roll in flour and season with salt and pepper. Place in tightly covered container to which one-half cup water has been added. Cook slowly in 325 degree oven until done (about two hours). Add water when needed. Vegetables like quartered carrots, potatoes and onions can be added when roast is about three-quarters done.

Chicken-fried venison steaks: Pound round steak thoroughly with edge of saucer or meat pounder. Dip steaks into mixture of two beaten eggs and two tablespoons of milk. Roll in cracker crumbs. Fry on medium heat.

Smothered venison steaks: Pound steaks thoroughly. Season with salt and pepper and roll in flour. Brown in pan to which one tablespoon of grease has been added. In another pan brown one medium diced onion, one-half medium green bell pepper, one sliced clove of garlic and a pinch of bay leaf. Add mixture to pan in which steaks have been browned along with one cup of water. Simmer slowly until done, or about one hour. Add water as needed.

Hot venison chili: Brown lightly two pounds of coarse ground venison in tablespoon of shortening. Add one tablespoon cut red pepper, one-half teaspoon Louisiana hot sauce, one-half teaspoon Worcestershire sauce, two medium, finely chopped onions, three-fourths of a finely chopped green bell pepper, one-fourth bay leaf, two small cans tomato paste, one No. 1 can of whole tomatoes, one teaspoon garlic powder and two tablespoons chili powder. Season to taste with salt and pepper. Allow to simmer for at least one-half day.

Deer fillets: Cut tenderloin in two-inch squares, one-half inch thick. Wrap with bacon and secure with toothpicks. Season with pepper and salt, or garlic salt can be substituted. Lay in open pan in which a sauce concocted of one large, finely chopped onion, one small can mushrooms and one small can mushroom gravy has been added. Cook in 325 degree oven, allowing meat to simmer in sauce, basting meat with sauce regularly. Allow from two to four fillets for each person served.

Deer sausage: Mix ratio of 40 per cent venison and 60 per cent pork. Season to taste with salt and coarsely ground pepper. Stuff and smoke lightly.

Deerburgers: Add one part pork to every four parts of venison. One part fat beef also can be added, if desired. Mash into large patties and grill over charcoal fire with hickory chips added. Barbecue sauce can be used for basting, or meat can be basted with melted margarine to prevent dryness and shrinkage.

Venison finger steaks: Cut tenderloin into thinnest strips possible. Soak for two hours in salt brine to draw out excessive blood. Drain thoroughly on paper towels. Brown and drop in deep pan of sizzling hot grease. Cook for thirty seconds to one minute, or until golden brown. Don't overcook.

Fried venison liver: Slice in thin steaks, roll in cornmeal, salt and pepper and fry in hot grease.

Smothered venison liver: Slice in thin steaks, roll in flour, salt and pepper, and brown in one tablespoon of shortening. Add enough water to cover meat along with two sliced medium onions. Simmer until tender, or about one hour.

17 The Camp

HALF THE fun of deer hunting is camping out, getting away from the hustle and bustle of everyday routine. Of course, in deer hunting it isn't necessary to "rough it." If the hunter so pleases, he can live in the luxurious comfort of a motel or hotel and drive to his hunting grounds each day. In prime deer country, good hunting is within a short drive of many rural villages.

But a good deer camp will get you more deer. The primary reason is that you can get far back in remote areas and consequently limit your competition. A four-wheel-drive vehicle will let you take advantage of the many logging roads in our national wilderness areas and carry you back into superb deer-hunting terrain.

The Michigan Conservation Department calls the Upper Peninsula of that state "an unmined deer-hunting goldmine" simply because it is wilderness country that few people bother to hunt.

A deer camp doesn't need to be anything fancy. But it should be practical. The deer hunter who is alert and up to his job must be refreshed and well fed.

Deer hunting is like anything else. The most successful hunters are the ones who put out that extra effort. The rank-and-file deer hunters stick close to public roads; the inveterate, serious hunter gets as far into the backwoods as possible.

Some hunters construct semi-permanent camps where this is permitted. Perhaps it is nothing more than a crude frame building, maybe covered with tar paper to keep out the wind, with a stove and rough bunks inside. These camps are popular on private lands where an arrangement can be worked out with the landowner. Also, in some wilderness areas, agreements can be made with the state or federal government to build this kind of camp.

With the portable camp, such as a tent, it is wise to remember that in some areas such as national forests and timber company lands there are designated spots for camping and camps must be erected in these plots and no other place. Also some areas require camping permits. Be sure of your camp-

Hunters return with their deer to a well-kept camp in a Forest Service area along the Tellico River in Tennessee. They've pitched wall tents for shelter. The cook uses a permanent fireplace with grill. *Courtesy U. S. Forest Service*

Tarp lean-tos are favored by many hunters who want to travel light. With a fire burning in front, a tarp absorbs heat and makes a warm shelter on the coldest nights.

site before setting up a home away from home.

Camp life is a relaxing existence. I remember a season in the Lincoln National Forest of New Mexico when Carlos Moore, Oscar Brown and I couldn't seem to get a deer, no matter what we tried. But that was a memorable season for me if for no other reason than the enjoyable nights I spent in our camp. It was down in a canyon filled with towering pines and green spruce, near the village of Weed. There's something magic about lounging around a campfire, under a sky alive with stars, reliving the day's hunt, swapping stories about past hunts and simply taking life easy.

If you want to hear some far-out stories, just get around Newt Long's deer camp in the Ocala National Forest of central Florida. Newt is a superintendent with a construction firm and his job has carried him throughout the United States. He's hunted in many different places and he's got some wild tales of hunting to tell. Of course, we listeners don't believe all of them, but you can get away with stretching the truth a mite in a deer camp. Everybody expects it.

Some hunters are content to move into an area a day before the season opens and set up a makeshift camp. Perhaps they'll come in two or three days early to scout out the area and get this home away from home in ship-shape order. There are many little things to be done that will make a camp more liveable.

For one thing, there's the matter of a shelter. If you're going to backpack into a remote area, perhaps you'll make a tarp lean-to suffice. But if you're driving or going by horseback, I strongly recommend that you carry a shelter that is large enough to be comfortable. Spend a couple of days in a camp when the rain is pelting down, as I have, and you'll appreciate an adequate shelter.

There are many good tents on the market. Most are lightweight and easy to erect. My personal favorite is the largest Pop-Tent. This is an oval-shaped tent with a built-in floor that can simply be picked up and moved around since it is not pegged to the ground. The only drawback to it is size. For two men it is adequate, but it can't accommodate any more comfortably.

Other tents are the Baker, the wall, the explorer's and the umbrella types. The wall tent probably is the most practical for all-around use, although the Baker is another favorite of mine. It is best to shop around and pick something that suits your fancy. But remember to get it large enough. When you pick one you believe to be adequate, then go to the next largest size. You'll never regret it.

The site for your tent requires some thought. Select a spot that is well drained (if you're not in a designated campsite). Never, for instance, place your tent in the bottom of a draw where a sudden heavy rain will fill it with water. Put it near a good water supply. Even if you carry your own drinking water, you'll need water for myriad other purposes, such as washing dishes and personal use. Try to put it where it is reasonably protected from wind, yet in a spot where it will be exposed to as much warming sunlight as possible during the day. This is important in the northern reaches of the country where the temperature is apt to plummet during the hunting season.

If you're not inclined to "rough it," one of the convenient, portable camp units is recommended: self-contained campers, fold-up tent trailers, pickup campers and compact house trailers. The major drawback to such a unit is

A pickup camper is a home on wheels for these hunters on the arid New Mexico plains. The interior is equipped with a stove, electric lights, and foam-rubber beds—a luxurious way to live in the field.

the price. My personal selection for the best hunting rig is an 8½-foot camper on a half-ton pickup powered by four-wheel drive or at least compound (grandma) gear. You'll sacrifice room for maneuverability, but you can take this rig almost anywhere. Any of the others will suffice in camping sites near easily traveled roads.

A compact house trailer makes a comfortable camp for hunters who travel into easily accessible areas.

The single most important item in a deer camp, as far as I'm concerned, is the sleeping bag. I can weather a lot of discomforts, but to be up to par I require a good night's sleep. An acceptable sleeping bag should be sufficiently insulated to keep the inhabitant warm, waterproof and spacious. Down is the warmest of all filler material but also the most expensive. Most of the bags today are filled with some sort of synthetic material, usually Dacron or Acrilan. In most climates, a bag filled with four or five pounds of Dacron is sufficient, if the temperature doesn't dip too low. But even this type bag is comfortable in cold weather if you put on a suit of thermal insulated underwear before entering the bag. This practically doubles the insulation.

An air mattress or a compact foam rubber mattress makes sleeping much more comfortable and serves as insulation from ground chill. A cot isn't necessary unless you wish to get off the ground. The best cots are those made with aluminum frames and plastic which make them lightweight and compact. In colder weather some sort of insulation is needed between bag and ground, even if it is just several layers of newspaper.

The matter of food also commands some thought. It is said that a hunter with a full belly is an alert hunter. Hot meals give more pep and help to relax tired muscles. A tent stove is not necessary. For warmth, use a wall tent and build your fire near the entrance. For cooking, compact gasoline stoves can't be beat. If there is no premium on weight and space, such as when traveling by vehicle, by all means have at least a two-burner stove. You'll need it when making coffee and frying at the same time. If you cook over an open campfire, a wire grate slung over a rock fireplace will make the task easier.

For lighting purposes, one or two gasoline lanterns will suffice. Don't forget to carry extra fuel and extra mantles. Also have at least one flashlight for each hunter. This is an almost indispensable item.

One or two lightweight tarpaulins also serve many useful purposes around camp. Put one under your sleeping bag to keep out moisture. Toss one over the camp stove to protect it from rain and insects.

It is best to plan your menus in advance so that you'll have enough food, but won't be burdened with excessive supplies. For fresh meats, carry along one of the lightweight ice chests. Otherwise, the choice of groceries is pretty much a personal thing, depending on what you prefer. For light traveling, such as backpacking, the newer freeze-dry foods are lightweight, yet very tasty.

An axe is needed to supply firewood. If weight permits it, carry a full-sized axe. It is a rare convenience. You just can't do the same job with one of the smaller portable axes. And remember the hallmark of a good woodsman is a sharp axe and a sharp knife. A small honing stone is good insurance.

Also, if possible have a shovel along. Use it to dig drainage ditches around your shelter and to dig a latrine. Put the latrine at least fifty yards from camp. Also bury all your garbage and tin cans when you break camp, or, better yet, carry it with you.

You might also want to include a small bucksaw to be used in obtaining firewood. Maybe even a hatchet for doing smaller chores around camp. An oven which fits over the gasoline stove is another little luxury that makes camp life more enjoyable. A bucket is another item that will serve a lot of uses.

The type of camp should reflect your own needs and the climate of the country. The man camping out in the deer country of northeastern Oklahoma would require a different camp than would the deer hunter in Maine. In warmer climates perhaps a simple lean-to will suffice; but in cold, biting weather an enclosed tent would be a welcome addition. The idea is to have a comfortable camp. With all the modern camping conveniences available today, there is no need to sacrifice comfort. Why suffer unnecessarily?

18 When the Fever Hits

THE DOE came easing deliberately down the trail. From where I lay bent over in a blind constructed of rotting, stacked logs, I kept watching her intently. She was a full seventy-five yards away, traveling a course that would carry her within a dozen feet of my blind. Mentally, I had a point all picked out up the trail, perhaps twenty-five yards away. In my mind I had everything worked into a neat scheme. When the doe reached that fateful spot, I was going to ease up and drive a deadly razorhead-tipped arrow through her chest.

But sometimes the best-laid plans can go astray. . . .

My rancher friend Guy Clymer had directed me to this particular stand. On my Texas hunting license I was entitled to two buck deer and a "bonus" deer, which by law had to be a doe, an innovation in Texas deer hunting to aid in reducing overpopulation in some areas. I'd been fortunate to fill my buck quota, and with almost half the season remaining I was going to try and collect my bonus deer with bow-and-arrow.

I contacted Clymer who had many doe permits remaining on his ranch near the small community of Llano in central Texas. He invited me up. The following morning he drove me out a country lane in the pre-dawn darkness and stopped where an electrical power line crossed the road.

"Remember that stand of stacked logs we hunted turkeys out of last year?" he asked softly.

I nodded.

"Well, follow this power line into the pasture, heading into the wind. Down there in the creek bottom you'll come to that stand. Climb in it, lie low and wait. Chances are, a deer will come down that trail and you ought to get a decent shot."

I eased into the blind just as the landscape around me started to brighten. As the new day dawned still and crisp, the live-oak trees scattered through the creek bottom literally came to life. Fox squirrels ran back and forth in the treetops, fussing and barking.

130

How the doe got into the picture so silently and quickly, I'll never know. One moment I looked up at the squirrels playing in the trees; the next, I glanced up the trail and there stood the sleek animal, so statue-like that she didn't appear real.

The doe was standing and staring right at my blind. Had the movement of my head given me away? I tried to stifle my breathing, to remain as still and quiet as was humanly possible. The doe looked fixedly at my stand for probably thirty seconds; it seemed like eternity. Then with a swish-swash of her tail she started toward me again. After ten or twelve cautious steps she paused and looked once more.

The hand gripping my hunting bow became clammy. I wrapped the three fingers of my right hand tightly around the bow string and squeezed the nocked arrow to keep it from falling out of place. The suspense was maddening.

Walk, look, walk, look. That's the way she came, deliberately, slowly, pausing every few feet to survey all that was going on around her. I dared not move, afraid the restless shifting would reveal my presence.

Time seemed to stand still. Finally, the deer approached my mentally laid-out execution point. I gripped the bow even more tightly and started drawing the arrow back as I raised up ever so slowly, to get above the stacked logs for a shot.

I couldn't have planned it any better. The unalarmed doe turned and looked directly at me, frozen in a classic three-quarter pose, not flicking a single hair. I pulled the string back the length of the arrow, and that's when it hit . . . the dread fever. My arms began shaking violently, making the arrow tip jump as if it had come alive. I lost my composure and let the arrow go before I had regained full control. It veered in front of the deer and clattered harmlessly in the brush. The doe wheeled and jumped out of sight. I could see occasional glimpses of her white tail bobbing through the creek bottom.

Now I was really shaking. I went all to pieces. It was as if all my muscles, tied up in knots and tensed for so long, finally relaxed.

I'd been stricken by that old hunting malady called "buck fever." It's a temporary, uncontrollable disease which strikes at the most inopportune times, usually when you are just drawing down on a deer, during that moment of truth when your finger tightens on the trigger or you start pulling back on the bowstring.

When it happens you may as well laugh it off as just one of those things that can occur in hunting. Like Marvin Essex of Bardstown, Kentucky, did. This retired army officer came pulling a nice deer from the woods.

"Got 'im with one shot," he said.

"I thought I heard you shoot eleven times," said P. D. Johnson, his hunting companion.

"I did," Essex answered. "I shot once to attract the deer's attention, nine times to clear out the brush and once to kill him."

At the climax of action, when the trigger tightens, is the time buck fever is most prevalent. But it can strike swiftly, unexpectedly just about any time, when the hunter least expects it. At no time is the hunter really immune to it. And sometimes it can be drastic.

Like what happened to a hunter (no names, please) in northeastern Georgia. He was sitting up in the high fork of a treetop when this buck came wandering past. A well-placed, deliberate shot dropped the animal neatly. But then, as the deer fell, the fever hit. The hunter momentarily forgot he was in a tree. Jumping up, he ran toward the animal . . . right out into space. When searchers found him sometime later, he was clutching a broken leg, and not fifty feet away lay the dead deer.

The germs of buck fever penetrate the nervous system and emotion overcomes reasoning. And no hunter, notwithstanding his experience and age, is immune from the bugaboo. It can happen to the best of us.

Consider that deer my father missed two or three seasons back. He was sitting in a tree, on a board that had been hammered in a fork, overlooking a brushy draw while I worked around and tried to flush something in the open.

I was about halfway up the draw when I heard Dad shoot . . . once, twice. I ran ahead, confident he'd have a buck on the ground. But upon my arrival on the scene, he was still shaking his head in exasperation. The deer had slipped right up the draw as predicted, all right, but Dad had blown two easy chances. And the buck wasn't a trophy either, just an average six-pointer.

"I don't know what happened," Dad admitted. "I guess I just got a good case of buck fever."

It was quite a confession, coming from him. Dad has been hunting deer for more than forty-five years. He's bagged some truely outstanding trophies, so just killing a deer is no banner-waving experience to him. But Dad is an addicted deer hunter; he gets wrapped up in the sport emotionally. And when those sensitive emotions are brought into play, the hunter is susceptive to buck fever. Anything can happen.

Curiously, the persons who have a reputation for being super-duper deer hunters are often those most susceptive to buck ague. In the presence of others, they must "prove" their reputation is earned, not blown into myth by talk. This pressure often makes them think, to try and reason out each shot, and when the hunter starts thinking he is throwing his defenses open to the fever.

When the sight settles on the deer's vital area and the trigger finger starts applying pressure, every move should be instinctive, made without any forethought or doubt. If there is a twinge of doubt in the hunter's mind as to his own ability, then, brother, he really is exposing his vulnerable side to this dread disease of hunting.

A hunter does queer things when gripped by the fever. Like that incident which happened a few seasons back in Litchfield County, Connecticut. A friend of mine was telling me the story. Seems he took a neighbor of his, a novice at deer hunting, out to try and get him a buck. He sat the man down next to a big tree, told him to stay put and watch, and then he started working around in an attempt to drive a deer within gunshot range. He jumped an exceptionally large buck and noticed the critter was heading directly toward

Most hunters have to work for their deer, others just rely on luck. *Courtesy George X. Sand*

the spot where the hunter lay in wait, on a course as straight and true as if an engineer had laid it out.

My friend Ed Sparks listened for the anticipated shot. The silence was overpowering. Surely, he thought to himself, the hunter had seen the buck. He couldn't have avoided it.

When Ed got back to the hunter, the latter appeared to be in momentary shock. His eyes were wild-looking and glassy. Ed asked if he'd seen the buck. The hunter nodded his head weakly.

"Yeah, but I missed 'im with every shot," he gasped dejectedly.

Missed with every shot??!! Ed hadn't heard him shoot, not once. He looked down to the ground and there, sparkling in the sunlight, were five live cartridges. In his excitement, the hunter had jacked them out of the rifle without once pulling the trigger.

Another time, a friend of mine, who will remain anonymous for obvious reasons, and I had just unloaded our rifles in preparation for getting into the auto and driving to another spot when, shockingly, a nice buck suddenly trotted out of the trees roughly one hundred yards up from us and stopped in the middle of a large clearing.

My friend, his rifle still in his hands, fished frantically in his pocket for a cartridge. He came up with two, rammed them both into the magazine, and quickly pumped the rifle three times, throwing all three cartridges out, rested the rifle over the car door and carefully squeezed off a shot. Naturally, the firing pin clicked harmlessly.

In that moment of nerve-racking excitement, when game is sighted, just about anything can happen. But a man is even more likely to catch buck fever when he has a chance to wait and think. Perhaps he sees a buck lurking off in the bordering underbrush, moving around where there isn't a chance for a shot. The hunter sits impatiently, hoping the deer will eventually show itself. All the while, he has time to think about the circumstance, the way he's going to handle the situation should it be legal game, where he's going to put the bullet.

As his nerves screw up tightly, the fever really goes to work on him.

Once my dad and I were stalking through some heavy timber when I chanced to see a deer slipping through the growth. I grabbed Dad's arm and pulled him down into a squatting position, pointing to the animal moving in the cover. All we could see were feet and legs.

Dad leaned over and whispered in my ear: "Acts like a buck." He pointed with his finger. "When he crosses through that clearing be ready to blast him if you see horns."

I raised the gun to half mast and positioned my finger on the safety catch, all the while watching the moving legs with concentrated attention. The closer they approached to the clearing, the more clammy my hands felt, the more my muscles started to tense and quiver.

The deer eased into the opening, stopped and looked straight at us. It was a beautiful sight, the deer framed by the alley of trees, the antlers catching the sunlight. I couldn't have asked for an easier setup. The buck was less than forty yards away.

The sights settled just behind the shoulder. That's when the fever grabbed hold unmercifully. The sight pattern started to waver. Instead of waiting for a split-second to try and calm down, I panicked, hurrying my shot before the deer ran. I jerked the trigger instead of squeezing properly. The boom of the big gun reverberated through the woods, and the deer vanished.

I turned and looked at Dad soberly. He was trying awfully hard to stifle a grin.

"You should have seen that rifle barrel of yours," he chuckled. "It was waving all over the place."

It was a great letdown at the time, muffing the oh-so-easy chance. But it is experiences such as this which make deer hunting the rewarding sport it is. After all, the hunting of deer is just a fascinating challenge, a game. A man is supposed to hunt for the fun of it. If ever I should fail to get excited when a deer walks into my sights, then I'm going to hang up my rifle and call it quits. It no longer will be worth the bother.

Helpful Hints
for Deer Hunters

An alert deer might not become too alarmed at sounds which seem natural, like the snapping of a twig, but any unnatural noise such as cartridges jingling around in the hunter's pocket immediately signals danger to its sensitive ears. Eliminate this problem in several ways: carry spare ammo in store-bought cases, in a cartridge belt, in the finger of a spare pair of gloves, in one of those plastic cigarette packages, or bind them together with a rubber band.

Any broadhead hunting arrow, to be effective, must be razor sharp. Rust quickly dulls sharpened edges. Keep them sharp by rubbing with wax. The protective coating eliminates rust.

A handy rifle-cleaning rod for the deer camp can be improvised from a piece of rawhide. Slit one end to take a patch and draw through the bore.

For easy skinning of deer, hang the animal by antlers or head. This way the hide comes off with the lay of the ribs and flank muscles.

Offhand shooting is the biggest gamble in deer hunting. Whenever possible, always use a rest, even if you just drop to one knee and steady your elbow. A handy tree also affords a place to steady your rifle and makes bullet placement more of a sure thing.

If you plan on waiting to ambush your buck, carry along one of those compact, fold-up camp stools. Elevation keeps you off the chilled ground and makes stand hunting much more comfortable.

*

Rain or mist can fog up a scope sight and makes aiming difficult. Make a convenient lens cover by cutting a two-inch-wide band from an old rubber inner tube. The band fits over the scope ends, keeping rain out, yet it can be removed in a jiffy for quick shooting.

*

An axe with a naked blade lying carelessly around camp is inviting disaster. Cut a piece of old garden hose the width of the axe blade, slit one side and slip it over the edge. Two rubber bands will hold the protector tight over the blade.

*

In an emergency the dip stick of your vehicle will provide enough lubrication to oil your rifle in camp. Another handy gadget is a lamb's-wool pad saturated with oil sewed to the flap of your gun case. The pad holds oil for a long time and is always there to use.

*

When you store your rifle away after the deer season, grease the weapon liberally and then insert in an old discarded nylon stocking. Nylon keeps oil and grease from being rubbed off by interior of case.

*

Always check out familiar landmarks around camp before venturing into the woods. Later, they may lead you to safety.

*

If you should sight an unalarmed doe slipping across a clearing, wait and be patient. A buck may soon follow. The male habitually follows the female.

*

A fast way of breaking in a pair of new hunting boots prior to the season is to soak them for ten to fifteen minutes in water. Now wear the boots until they are completely dry.

When conducting a deer drive it is difficult to signal between hunters without making a lot of undue commotion and noise. One way is to carry an empty rifle cartridge. Blow into it for a shrill whistle. Makes a nifty signaling device, yet it won't alarm deer.

✳

Ever gone to deer camp, bagged your deer opening day, then had to wait around while your companions got theirs? Next time carry along a copy of your local game laws. Perhaps there is other game in season and you can spend your time hunting rather than waiting.

✳

If you buy a new rifle that's shorter than the old one and it won't fit in the gun case, don't despair. Just stuff the barrel end of the case with old rags until you get a snug fit.

✳

If you prefer a back or belt quiver to carry your hunting arrows, try wrapping the broadheads individually in newspaper before inserting the arrows into the quiver. The paper will prevent unnecessary noise and will keep the heads from rubbing together and becoming dull.

✳

Hunting boots can be quickly laced in camp, even with cold fingers, if you first char the ends of the laces with a match flame.

✳

One of the hardest parts of camp life is getting up in the cold of pre-dawn and attempting to get a fire going with soggy wood. Eliminate this by laying out your fire the previous night, then covering with a piece of tarp or plastic. The next morning the wood will be set up and dry, quickly lighted.

✳

Boot laces have the maddening habit of becoming untied as you hunt, catching on bushes and briers. Prevent this by tying twice. Lace up, tie in conventional manner, then take the loop ends and knot them together. Laces won't come loose.

✳

When approaching a fallen buck, come up from the back and nudge it with your rifle barrel to make sure it is dead. Otherwise, the deer might rare up and lunge into you.

*

Never bring a loaded weapon into camp. Always keep the safety intact until you are ready to shoot. Always be doubly sure of your target before pulling the trigger. The careless hunter will soon find that he has no *friends* to hunt with.

*

A spare mantle for your camp lantern is good insurance. Tape one to the bottom of the lantern. It will always be handy in an emergency.

*

Every deer hunter operates more efficiently if he has a hot meal under his belt. But who wants the thankless chore of keeping the camping utensils clean? It is a job that must be done and you can make it easier by covering the bottom of pots and coffee makers with aluminum foil. When you're finished the foil can be removed and your utensils will look like new.

*

Waterproof matches are good insurance should you become lost. Make up some in a jiffy by dipping the heads in your wife's nail polish. If you have a waterproof match box, cut the stems in half. The box will hold twice as many matches this way.

*

Ordinary furniture polish rubbed on rifle stocks will keep them shiny and new looking.

*

To eliminate glare from open iron sights, just run a lighted match over each sight. The carbon deposit eliminates the glare.

*

When storing away your leather hunting boots, stuff them with newspaper. Paper helps the boots retain their shapes, keeps wrinkles and creases out, and prolongs life of boots.

Record Whitetail Deer

TYPICAL

Score	*Locality Killed*	*Date Killed*	*By Whom Killed*	*Owner*	*Rank*
202	Funkley, Minn.	1918	John A. Breen	Arthur, Harry and Ray Breen	1
198 3/8	Allegany Co., N.Y.	1939	Roosevelt Luckey	N.Y. Conservation Dept.	2
193 6/8	Christopher Lake, Saskatchewan	1959	Jerry Thorson	Jerry Thorson	3
191 5/8	Flathead County, Montana	1963	Earl McMaster	Earl McMaster	4
190	Dimmitt Co., Texas	1950	C. P. Howard	C. P. Howard	5

NON-TYPICAL

149:137=286	McCulloch Co., Texas	1892	Jeff Benson	Lone Star Brewing Co.	1
185 7/8:91 4/8= 277 3/8	Hall Co., Nebraska	1962	Del Austin	Del Austin	2
191 5/8:54 2/8= 245 7/8	Elk River, British Columbia	1905	James I. Brewster	James I. Brewster Estate	3
174 3/8:71 1/8= 245 4/8	Carrot River, Saskatchewan	1962	Picked Up	Ken. Halloway	4
208 2/8:35 3/8= 243 5/8	Govan, Saskatchewan	1951	A. W. Davis	Lund's Wildlife Exhibit	5

COUES DEER

143	Pima Co., Ariz.	1953	Ed Stockwell	Ed Stockwell	1
133 3/8	Burro Creek, Ariz.	1950	Noel Scott	Noel Scott	2
131 7/8	Huachuca Mts., Ariz.	1935	George W. Kouts	George W. Kouts	3
125 4/8	Arivaca, Ariz.	1953	Gerald Harris	Gerald Harris	4
124 5/8	Rincon Mts., Ariz.	1936	James Pfersdorf	Mrs. J. E. Pfersdorf, Sr.	5

From *Records of North American Big Game* by the Boone and Crockett Club, published by Holt, Rinehart and Winston.

INDEX